I0225623

Conceptual Foundations of Language Science

No scientific work proceeds without conceptual foundations. In language science, our concepts about language determine our assumptions, direct our attention, and guide our hypotheses and our reasoning. Only with clarity about conceptual foundations can we pose coherent research questions, design critical experiments, and collect crucial data. This series publishes short and accessible books that explore well-defined topics in the conceptual foundations of language science. The series provides a venue for conceptual arguments and explorations that do not require the traditional book-length treatment, yet that demand more space than a typical journal article allows.

In this series:

1. Enfield, N. J. *Natural causes of language*.

2. Müller, Stefan. *A lexicalist account of argument structure: Template-based phrasal LFG approaches and a lexical HPSG alternative*

ISSN: 2363-877X

A lexicalist account of argument structure

Template-based phrasal LFG approaches and a lexical HPSG alternative

Stefan Müller

Stefan Müller. 2018. *A lexicalist account of argument structure: Template-based phrasal LFG approaches and a lexical HPSG alternative* (Conceptual Foundations of Language Science 2). Berlin: Language Science Press.

This title can be downloaded at:
http://langsci-press.org/catalog/book/163

ISBN: 978-3-96110-121-4 (Digital)
978-3-96110-122-1 (Hardcover)

ISSN: 2363-877X
DOI:10.5281/zenodo.1441351
Source code available from www.github.com/langsci/163
Collaborative reading: paperhive.org/documents/remote?type=langsci&id=163

Cover and concept of design: Ulrike Harbort
Typesetting: Stefan Müller
Proofreading: Barend Beekhuizen, Mykel Brinkerhoff, Aniefon Daniel, Gerald Delahunty, Bojana Đorđević Andreas Hölzl, Ivica Jeđud, Vadim Kimmelman, Timm Lichte, Joey Lovestrand, Valeria Quochi, Janina Rado, Brett Reynolds, Alexandr Rosen, Ivelina Stoyanova, Jeroen van de Weijer, Alena Witzlack-Makarevich, Annie Zaenen
Fonts: Linux Libertine, Libertinus Math, Arimo, DejaVu Sans Mono
Typesetting software: XƎLaTeX

Language Science Press
Unter den Linden 6
10099 Berlin, Germany
langsci-press.org

Storage and cataloguing done by FU Berlin

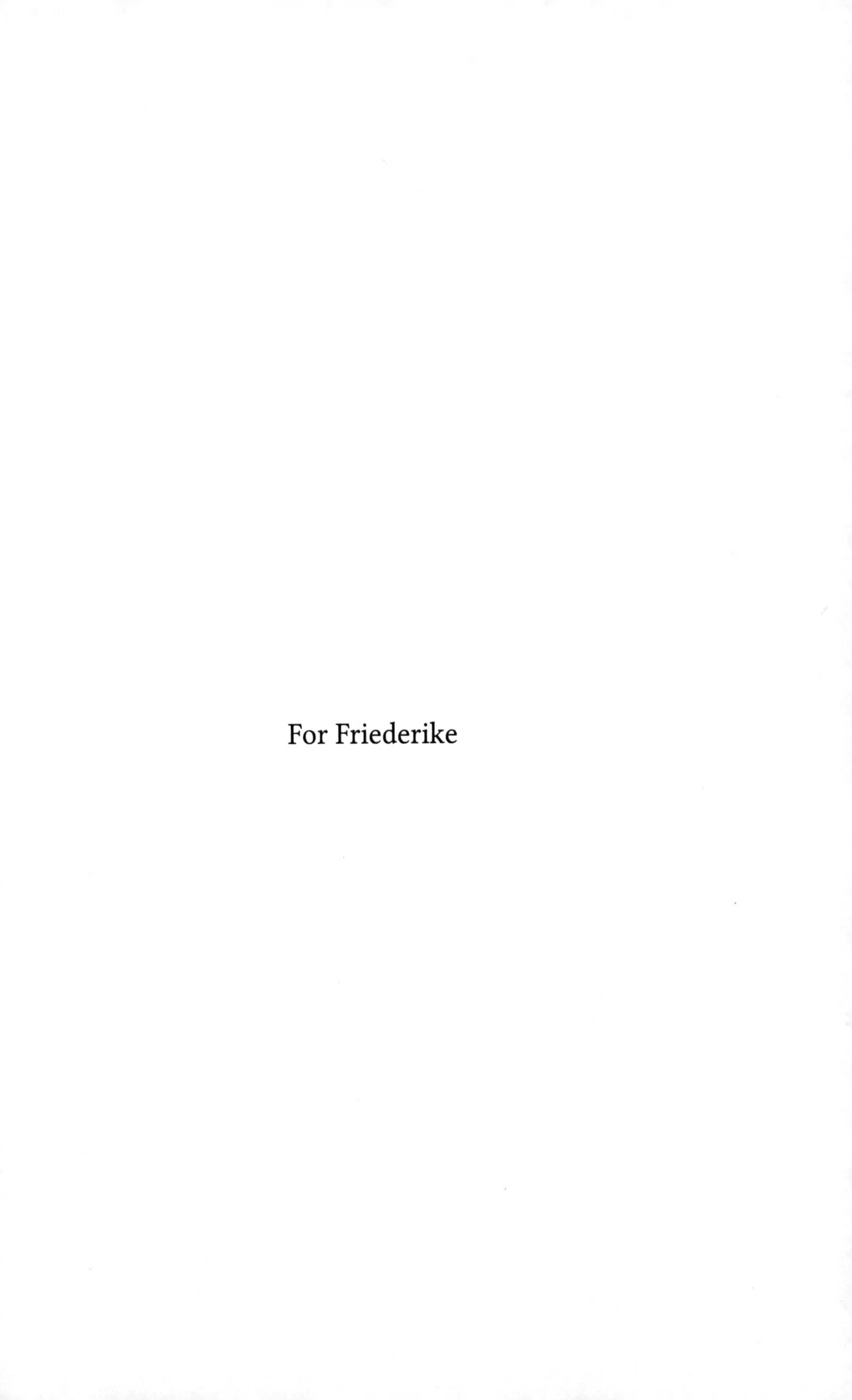

For Friederike

Contents

Preface

This book is part of my efforts to convince Construction Grammarians and people working in related frameworks that lexical approaches to argument structure are the only ones possible within a certain set of basic assumptions. I started this discussion with Kerstin Fischer and Anatol Stefanowitch 15 years ago in Bremen and continued it with friends and colleagues in the DFG-financed Construction Grammar network. Several publications grew out of this work (Müller 2006; 2007b; 2010b; Müller & Wechsler 2014a,b; 2015; Müller 2016b; 2017b). Usually the proposals I argued against were not formalized and/or the phenomena I pointed out as problematic were not covered in theoretical work so far. This is different for the present book: the constructional proposals I discuss are formulated in Lexical Functional Grammar. Most of the phenomena are covered and one can clearly see consequences of the proposals I discuss. The book does not only discuss a constructional LFG analysis of benefactive constructions, it also provides an alternative lexical HPSG analysis that also shows how interactions of benefactives with resultative constructions and passive and derivational morphology can be covered in a way that allows for cross-linguistic generalizations. The HPSG analysis is implemented in the TRALE system (Meurers, Penn & Richter 2002; Penn 2004) as part of the CoreGram project (Müller 2015b) and will be part of the Grammix Virtual Machine (Müller 2007c).

Acknowledgments

I thank Ash Asudeh for a really detailed discussion of an earlier version of this book and of Asudeh et al. (2014). I thank Ida Toivonen for discussion of Toivonen (2013) and Asudeh et al. (2014) via email. I am very grateful for the LaTeX sources Ash provided for the proofs and figures that I quoted from their paper. This saved me a lot of time! I want to also thank Elizabeth Christie for providing the LaTeX code for a lexical item.

I thank Steve Wechsler for discussion of an earlier version of this book. Thanks to Jonas Kuhn for discussion of the attachment of constraints to c-structures and Economy of Expression.

I also want to thank the participants of HeadLex 2016, the joint conference on LFG and HPSG, for (intense) discussion. Miriam Butt, Mary Dalrymple, Ron Kaplan, and Anna Kibort deserve special mention.

Thanks also goes to Martin Haspelmath and Adam Przepiórkowski for comments on an earlier version of this book.

Furthermore, I thank Gert Webelhuth, Gerald Penn, Tom Wasow, Paul Kay, Adele Goldberg, Jean-Pierre Koenig, Doug Arnold, Aaron Broadwell, and Berthold Crysmann for various comments and pointers to relevant literature.

A five page abstract was submitted to HeadLex 2016. I am grateful to the reviewers of this abstract and the reviewers of a revised 20 page version. I also thank Miriam Butt and Tracy Holloway King for comments on and discussion of the proceedings version. The comments helped a lot to shape and improve this book. Thanks!

This book underwent community proofreading and I want to thank the proofreaders (Barend Beekhuizen, Mykel Brinkerhoff, Aniefon Daniel, Gerald Delahunty, Bojana Đorđević Andreas Hölzl, Ivica Jeđud, Vadim Kimmelman, Timm Lichte, Joey Lovestrand, Valeria Quochi, Janina Rado, Brett Reynolds, Alexandr Rosen, Ivelina Stoyanova, Jeroen van de Weijer, Alena Witzlack-Makarevich, Annie Zaenen) for their careful work: you did an amazing job and Annie Zanen and Timm Lichte even commented on content. Thanks!

Berlin, 18th October 2018 Stefan Müller

1 Introduction

This book argues that argument structure should be treated lexically rather than as fixed phrasal configurations. This is discussed with respect to the benefactive construction and the resultative construction. It is shown that both constructions are more flexible than claimed in previous publications and that generalizations about the construction cannot be captured language internally and cross-linguistically in phrasal approaches. This first chapter is intended to introduce the reader to the history and current form of the phrasal/lexical debate.

Currently, there are two big camps in grammatical theory: the Chomskyan research tradition (Chomsky 1981; 1995) going back to earlier work by Chomsky (1957) and the more recent framework of Construction Grammar (CxG, Fillmore, Kay & O'Connor 1988; Goldberg 1995; 2006; Tomasello 2003).[1] Within the Chomskyan research tradition, *Lectures on Government & Binding* was very influential (Chomsky 1981). It initiated a lot of research, both in syntax and in language acquisition. Starting with Chomsky (1973) and Jackendoff (1977), restrictive models of constituent structure were assumed stating that all constituents that are licensed by a core grammar have the format determined by $\overline{\text{X}}$ schemata. It was argued that there is a Poverty of the Stimulus from which it follows that there has to be innate domain-specific knowledge about linguistics (Universal Grammar, UG). The part of the grammar that is acquired with the help of this UG is called the core grammar. The rest being the so-called periphery. The $\overline{\text{X}}$ schemata are rather abstract rules that state that a head combines with its complements to

[1]The series editors asked me to modify this sentence since I would run the risk of annoying my readers on the first page of my book by stating that there are just two big camps in grammatical theory. I decided to leave the statement as is since I think it is the truth. I believe that I can make such a statement since I am working in a minority framework myself (Head-Driven Phrase Structure Grammar). I discussed various theoretical frameworks (Categorial Grammar, Generalized Phrase Structure Grammar, Lexical Functional Grammar, Tree Adjoining Grammar, Dependency Grammar) in Müller (2018b). Mainstream Generative Grammar (GB/Minimalism) and Construction Grammar differ from all other frameworks discussed in the book and smaller ones that could not be discussed in having various journals and book series exclusively dedicated to research within GB/Minimalism and CxG and in the number and size of conferences. A further difference is the number of chairs world wide and the number of grant applications per framework.

form an intermediate projection (1a) to which adjuncts may be added (1b). When a specifier is added a maximal projection (a complete phrase = XP) results (1c).

(1) a. XP → UP $\overline{\mathrm{X}}$
    b. $\overline{\mathrm{X}}$ → $\overline{\mathrm{X}}$ YP
    c. $\overline{\mathrm{X}}$ → X ZP

In addition to such abstract rules, general principles were assumed. The principles were formulated in a way that was general enough to make them work for all languages. The differences between languages were explained with references to parameters that could be set appropriately for a given language or language class. The parameters were assumed to be each responsible for a variety of phenomena so that the fixation of one parameter helped children to infer a lot of properties in one go and hence make language acquisition possible despite the alleged Poverty of the Stimulus. This general framework was very fruitful and inspired a lot of comparative work. However, it was realized pretty soon that switch-like parameters cannot be found: it is not the case that a abundance of phenomena is connected crosslinguistically (Haider 1994, 2001: Section 2.2; Müller 2016a: Section 16.1). There are tendencies, for sure, but no hard switch-like parameters that work exceptionless for all languages. Furthermore, it has been pointed out that there are no abrupt changes in language acquisition, something that would be expected if language acquisition would involve setting binary parameters (Bloom 1993: 731; Haider 1993: 6; Abney 1996: 3; Ackerman & Webelhuth 1998: Section 9.1; Tomasello 2000; 2003).

Another problem with the GB conception of Principles & Parameters is that the assumed UG is quite rich: it contains the principles (Case Assignment, Empty Category Principle, Extended Projection Principle, Subjacency) and on top of this grammatical categories and features, which have to be part of UG since the principles or the parameters refer to such information. Chomsky's Minimalist Program addressed the question of how information about such a rich UG is supposed to become part of the human genome and it was suggested that what is really part of the human genome is the ability to form recursive structures (Hauser, Chomsky & Fitch 2002). There have been several modifications to the rules and the basic machinery that is assumed and currently there are two basic operations left: External and Internal Merge (Chomsky 2001). External Merge combines a head with an argument and Internal Merge deletes a constituent in an existing tree and attaches it at the left periphery.

The Chomskyan division of Core and Periphery was criticized by proponents of Construction Grammar and the related Simpler Syntax since it was pointed out that a large part of our linguistic knowledge would be assigned to the Periphery. Now, if we are able to acquire the Periphery, which is by definition the irregular part of our linguistic systems, why shouldn't we be able to acquire the more regular parts of the Core? And, indeed, recent advances in statistical methods show that input-based learning is very likely to be sufficient for language acquisition: statistics-based determination of part of speech information is quite successful and Bod (2009) showed how syntactic structure and in particular auxiliary inversion, Chomsky's standard example in Poverty of the Stimulus discussions, can be learned from data without running in any Poverty of the Stimulus problems. The simulations by the group around Freudenthal yielded better explanations of language acquisition phenomena than earlier generative accounts (Freudenthal et al. 2007).

So, Construction Grammarians assume an input-based acquisition of language and reject the assumption of innate language-specific knowledge. It is assumed that language acquisition works via generalization over patterns. For instance, Tomasello (2003) assumes a transitive construction consisting of a subject, verb, and object:

(2) [Subj TrVerb Obj]

This can be seen as the generalization over various usage events involving transitive verbs like those in (3):

(3) a. [$_S$ [$_{NP}$ The man/the woman] sees [$_{NP}$ the dog/the rabbit/it]].
b. [$_S$ [$_{NP}$ The man/the woman] likes [$_{NP}$ the dog/the rabbit/it]].
c. [$_S$ [$_{NP}$ The man/the woman] kicks [$_{NP}$ the dog/the rabbit/it]].

While researchers like Croft (2001) and Tomasello (2003) see the pattern in (2) as the result of the generalization process other researchers assign more structure to sentences with transitive verbs and assume a VP. Nevertheless, it is obvious that Construction Grammar analyses are rather close to observable data and that most CxG analyses assume phrasal schemata like (2).

The following figures show the analysis of (4) in Minimalism and in Construction Grammar.

(4) Anna reads the book.

The analysis in Figure 1.1 is a completely flat structure as assumed by Croft and the one in Figure 1.2 is an analysis with VP as it is assumed in Sign-Based Construction Grammar and the analysis in Figure 1.3 is the Minimalist analysis in the version of Adger (2003). As is obvious, the Minimalist analysis is much more

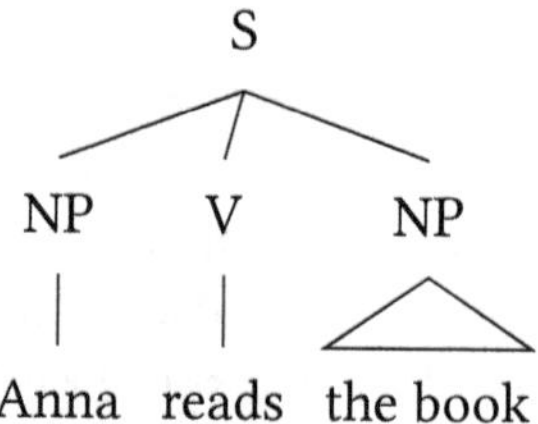

Figure 1.1: Analysis of *Anna reads the book.* in CxG according to Croft (2001)

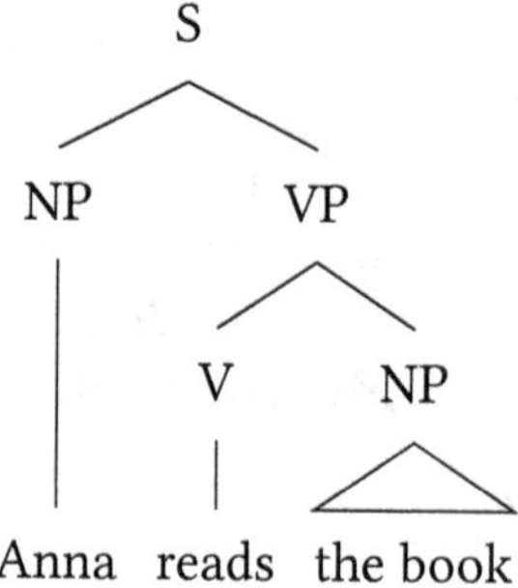

Figure 1.2: Analysis of *Anna reads the book.* in Sign-Based CxG according to Sag (2012)

complex. It involves additional categories like T and *v*. On the other hand the combinatorical operations (Merge) are very simple: two constituents are combined. Which elements are possible in such binary combinations is determined by features. For instance, verbs have features that correspond to the valence information known from other theories (e.g., LFG and HPSG).

The general debate is whether such structures can be learned or whether flat or flatter structures have to be assumed. Another issue is whether syntax is something involving abstract algorithmic rules like Move and Merge or whether syntax is a set of construction-specific rules that are combined with meaning. Semantics plays an important role in language acquisition. Work in GB and Minimalism usually deals with syntax only and ignores semantics, an exception being work in the Cartographic tradition of Rizzi (1997). In the latter type of work, information of all levels is syntactified, and we find semantic categories like Agent and Patient and information structure categories like Topic and Focus as node labels in syntactic trees. In Construction Grammar, on the other hand, there is the claim that every construction comes with a certain meaning. Therefore, syntax

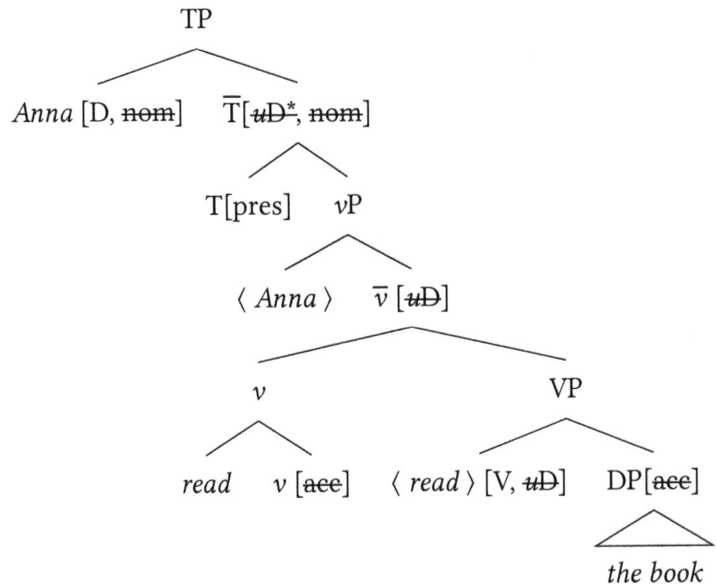

Figure 1.3: Minimalist analysis of *Anna reads the book.* according to Adger (2003)

and semantics are often treated simultaneously. This is also true for related theories like Head-Driven Phrase Structure Grammar (HPSG, Pollard & Sag (1987; 1994); Sag (1997)), which I am assuming here. Construction Grammar assumes that grammar is basically a set of form-meaning pairs. Lexical items, phrasal schemata, lexical rules are all form-meaning pairs. A special case of construction are so-called *argument structure constructions*[2]. The term *argument structure construction* refers to some theoretical entity (lexical item, lexical rule, phrase structure rule or schema) that licenses arguments. Depending on the authors, argument structure constructions can be lexical or phrasal constructions. This book is a contribution to the question of how argument structure constructions should be treated. While Minimalism assumes that heads select for arguments and abstract rules combine heads with arguments, most researchers working in Construction Grammar assume that there are very specific constructions that contribute meaning and license arguments. In what follows, I will introduce the specific topic of this book in a bit more detail. As I will show, the question is not just Minimalism vs. Construction Grammar since there are other theories that

[2]The term *argument structure construction* is an established term in Construction Grammar research. See, for instance, some of the paper and book titles in the list of references.

differ considerably from Minimalism, but nevertheless assume rich lexical items and very abstract combinatorical schemata. So the question of how arguments and heads should be represented and combined is a very central one that affects many linguistic frameworks.

Goldberg (1995; 2006), Tomasello (2003) and others argue for a phrasal view of argument structure constructions: lexical entries for verbs come with minimal specifications as to which arguments are required by a verb, but they come with a specification of argument roles. Verbs can be inserted into phrasal constructions, and these constructions may express the arguments that belong to a verb semantically or even add further arguments. A frequently discussed example is the one in (5):

(5) He runs his sneakers threadbare.

run is an intransitive verb, but, in (5), it enters the resultative construction, which licenses an additional argument (*his sneakers*) and a result predicate (*threadbare*). The resultative semantics is said to be contributed by the whole phrasal pattern rather than by one of its elements (for instance, Goldberg, 1991: 88–89; 1995; Goldberg & Jackendoff (2004: 533)). The lexical approach assumes that there are several lexical items for verbs like *run*. There is the lexical item that is needed to analyze simple sentences with the intransitive verb and its subject, and there is a further lexical item that is used in the analysis of sentences like (5). The latter lexical item selects for a subject, an object and a result predicate and contributes the resultative semantics. Both lexical items are usually related by a lexical rule. See Simpson (1983), Verspoor (1997), Wechsler (1997), Wechsler & Noh (2001), Wunderlich 1992: 45; 1997: 120–126, Kaufmann & Wunderlich (1998), Müller (2002: Chapter 5), and Christie (2015) for lexical analyses in several frameworks.

Lexical approaches usually assume abstract rules or schemata for the combination of lexical items. For instance, Categorial Grammar assumes functional application and Minimalism assumes Merge. Head-Driven Phrase Structure Grammar has a Head-Complement Schema and a Specifier-Head Schema. These abstract schemata are assumed to provide minimal semantic information (functional application) but do not add any construction-specific semantics. Construction Grammar proposals like the one of Tomasello and the one of Goldberg come with strong claims about the non-existence of such abstract rules (Tomasello 2003: 99). They argue with respect to language acquisition that all constructions are phrasal and that what is acquired is phrasal patterns. As is shown in Müller (2010a: Section 11.11.8.1), Müller (2016a) and Müller & Wechsler (2014a: Section 9.1), phrasal constructions cannot be the result of language acquisition, it is rather dependencies that are important for the characterization of the linguistic knowledge of competent speakers. This book argues that both phrasal constructions in the sense of Construction Grammar and abstract schemata in the sense of Categorial Grammar, HPSG and Minimalism are needed. Hence, it argues for a broader view on language that incorporates insights from both schools and fuses them into a new, unified framework.

The question, whether constructions like (5) should be treated as lexical or as phrasal constructions, has been discussed in the literature in several papers (Goldberg & Jackendoff 2004; Müller 2006; Goldberg 2013b; Müller & Wechsler 2014a) but since most Construction Grammar publications (intentionally, see Goldberg (2006: Section 10.4)) are not formalized, the discussion of aspects not treated in the original proposal (e.g., interaction with morphology, application of the approach to non-configurational languages like German, partial verb phrase fronting) was rather hypothetical. There have been Construction Grammar-inspired proposals in HPSG (Haugereid 2007; 2009) and Simpler Syntax (Culicover & Jackendoff 2005) and these were shown to have empirical problems, to make wrong predictions or to be not extendable to other languages (Müller 2013b; 2016a). Formal CxG proposals (Bergen & Chang 2005; van Trijp 2011) are discussed in Müller (2016a: Chapter 10.6.3) and Müller (2017c).[3] Recently, several articles have been published suggesting a template-based phrasal approach in LFG that makes use of glue semantics, a resource-driven semantic theory (Christie 2010; Asudeh, Giorgolo & Toivonen 2014). While these proposals seem to avoid many of the challenges that earlier proposals faced, they, in fact, have many of the problems that were discussed with respect to hypothetical extensions of non-formal proposals in Construction Grammar. Fortunately, the LFG proposals are worked out in detail and are embedded in a formal theory that provides formalized analyses of the languages and phenomena under discussion. It is, therefore, possible to show what the new template-based theories predict and to pin down exactly the phenomena where they fail.

The traditional analysis of the resultative construction in the framework of LFG is a lexical one (Simpson 1983), but, more recently, several researchers have suggested a different view on certain argument structure constructions in the framework of LFG. For instance, Alsina (1996) and Christie (2010) suggest analyzing resultative constructions as phrasal constructions and Asudeh, Dalrymple

[3]Sign-Based Construction Grammar (SBCG) is also formalized, but SBCG assumes a lexical approach to argument structure constructions. Sag, Boas & Kay (2012) are very explicit about this being a fundamental property of SBCG and they cite Müller (2006) and Müller (2010b) on this. SBCG is a HPSG variant (Sag (2010: 486); Müller (2016a: Section 10.6.2)) and hence it is no surprise that it is fully compatible with what is argued for in this book.

& Toivonen (2008; 2013) argue for a phrasal analysis of the (Swedish) caused motion construction. Toivonen (2013) discusses benefactive constructions of the type in (6b):

(6) a. The performer sang a song.
    b. The performer sang the children a song.

Toivonen notices that the benefactive NP cannot be fronted in questions (7) and that passivization is excluded for some speakers of English (8).[4]

(7) a. I baked Linda cookies.
    b. * Who did I bake cookies?
    c. The kids drew their teacher a picture.
    d. * Which teacher did the kids draw a picture?

(8) * My sister was carved a soap statue of Bugs Bunny (by a famous sculptor).

While Toivonen provides a lexical rule-based analysis of benefactives in her 2013 paper, she states in the discussion section:

> The manipulations that involve the word order consistently render the examples ungrammatical; see section 2.3 for the relative ordering test, section 2.4 and examples (47–48) for wh-extraction, section 2.5 for VP anaphora, and section 2.6 for pseudo-clefts. The distribution of benefactive NPs is thus very limited: it can only occur in the frame given in (5). This does not directly follow from the analysis given in section 3, and I will not attempt to offer an explanation for these intriguing facts here. However, it is perhaps possible to adopt an analysis similar to the one Asudeh et al. (2013) propose for the Swedish directed motion construction (Toivonen 2002). Asudeh et al. (2013) posit a template that is directly associated with a construction-specific phrase structure rule. (Toivonen 2013: 516)

The configuration that she provides in her (5) is given in Figure 1.4 on the facing page here. Asudeh, Giorgolo & Toivonen (2014) develop the respective phrasal analysis of the benefactive construction.

Note that Asudeh, Dalrymple, and Toivonen do not argue for a phrasal treatment of argument structure constructions in general. They do not assume that

[4]See Hudson (1992: 257) for references to several papers with varying judgments of question formation involving the fronting of the primary object. See Langendoen et al. (1973) for an experimental study.

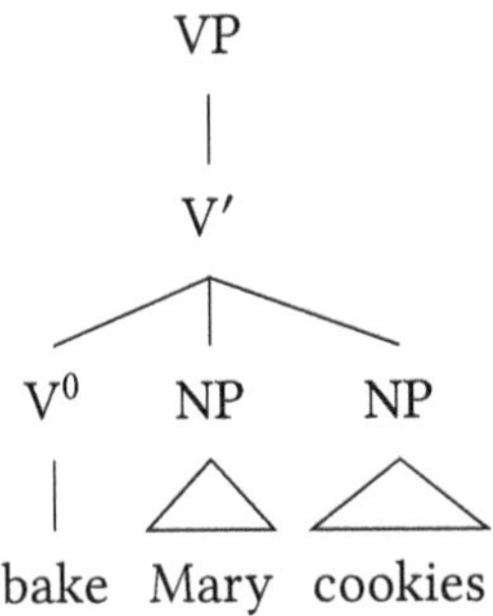

Figure 1.4: Phrasal configuration for benefactives according to Toivonen (2013: 505)

there is a phrasal transitive construction that licenses arguments for normal sentences like *Kim likes Sandy.* or a phrasal ditransitive construction that licenses the objects of normal ditransitive verbs like *give*. The authors continue to assume that the arguments of verbs like *like* and *give* are specified lexically. They just treat certain specific constructions phrasally, namely those that have a fixed conventionalized form or special idiosyncratic constraints on order that are difficult to capture lexically.

Nevertheless, the approach of Asudeh et al. (2014) could be seen as a way to formalize phrasal constructional approaches like those by Goldberg (1995; 2004) and Culicover & Jackendoff (2005). What I want to show in this book is that the phrasal LFG approach has too many drawbacks in comparison to the lexical approaches. Since the phrasal approach is rejected for two specific argument structure constructions (benefactives and resultatives), it follows that it cannot be a viable approach for all argument structure constructions. So even though Christie and Asudeh et. al. do not assume that all argument structure constructions should be handled as in phrasal Construction Grammar, these two proposals for two specific phrasal constructions can be used to show the problems that approaches have that treat all argument structure constructions as phrasal constructions.[5]

Another note of caution is necessary here. This book is not a book against Construction Grammar. There are many versions of Construction Grammar. Most assume a phrasal treatment of argument structure constructions (Tomasello 2003;

[5]It is clear that other variants of the phrasal approach could exist in principle. It is difficult to prove that all imaginable variants of the phrasal approach run into problems. But the phenomena and their interaction discussed in this book can serve as a benchmark for alternative phrasal theories that may be developed in the future.

Goldberg 1995; 2006; Goldberg & Jackendoff 2004; Bergen & Chang 2005; van Trijp 2011), but there are variants like Berkeley Construction Grammar (Kay 2005) and Sign-Based Construction Grammar (SBCG, Sag, Boas & Kay 2012) that are explicitly lexical. (See also Croft (2003) and Goldberg (2013a) for discussions of lexical and phrasal constructional approaches.) The proposal I work out in this book in the framework of Constructional Head-Driven Phrase Structure Grammar (Constructional HPSG, Sag 1997) is a lexical constructional proposal. It is equivalent to what would be done in SBCG, which comes with no big surprise since SBCG is a variant of HPSG (Sag 2010: 486).

I also do not argue against the attachment of templates to c-structure rules. In fact, it is good to have this possibility. Such annotated c-structure rules can be used to describe phrasal constructions in which no plausible head can be identified as, for instance, Jackendoff's N-P-N construction (2008), which is exemplified in (9):

(9) student after student

Since – as Jackendoff argued in detail – no element of this phrase can plausibly be seen as the head there is no element that could be seen as responsible for the internal structure of the phrase. Therefore, there is no non-ad hoc lexical item to attach constraints to and attaching templates to a c-structure seems to be the only option.

This book is structured as follows: Chapter 2 introduces the template-based phrasal approach. I then discuss interactions of the resultative and benefactive construction with extraction, passivization and coordination (Chapter 3). Chapter 4 is devoted to requirements of morphological processes. I then go on to discuss possible treatments of passivization and point out that generalizations are missed language internally (Chapter 5). Chapter 6 examines how the analyses could be adapted to German and I argue that cross-linguistic generalizations are not captured in phrasal analyses. Chapter 7 develops a lexical approach in the framework of HPSG, explains how cross-linguistic generalizations – including generalizations regarding constituent structure – can be captured and shows how restrictions on extraction and passivization can be captured in a lexical analysis. The book concludes in Chapter 8.

2 The template-based approach

This section introduces two phrasal approaches in more detail. Both approaches are based on templates (Dalrymple et al. 2004), glue semantics (Dalrymple 1999), and a version of the Lexical Mapping Theory (Bresnan & Kanerva 1989; Kibort 2008). Glue semantics is interesting since logical formulae are resource sensitive; that is, certain items have to be consumed during a semantic combination. This sort of consumption can be used to model valence. I start with the treatment of benefactives in Asudeh et al. (2014) in the following subsection and then turn to Christie's treatment of resultatives (2010).

2.1 Benefactive constructions

This subsection consists of two parts: I first explain the general assumptions made by template-based approaches using glue semantics and then comment on why this is different from earlier inheritance-based proposals and explain why certain problems do not arise and which problems are left.

2.1.1 General assumptions and the Benefactive template

Figure 2.1 shows the analysis of (10) that is assumed by Asudeh et al. (2014: 75):

(10) Kim ate at noon.

There is a constituent structure (c-structure) that is related via the function ϕ to a functional structure (f-structure), which is in turn related to a semantic structure (s-structure) via a further function σ. The s-structure is a new semantic level that is supposed to fulfill the function of the argument structure representation (a-structure) that is usually assumed in versions of LFG that rely on Lexical Mapping Theory (Bresnan & Zaenen 1990; Bresnan et al. 2015: Chapter 14).

The authors follow a neo-Davidsonian approach, that is, verbs introduce a one-place predicate that takes an event as its sole argument. Further argument roles can be added as predicating of the same event. For instance, the meaning of *Kim ate* in (10) is represented as (11), ignoring tense information.

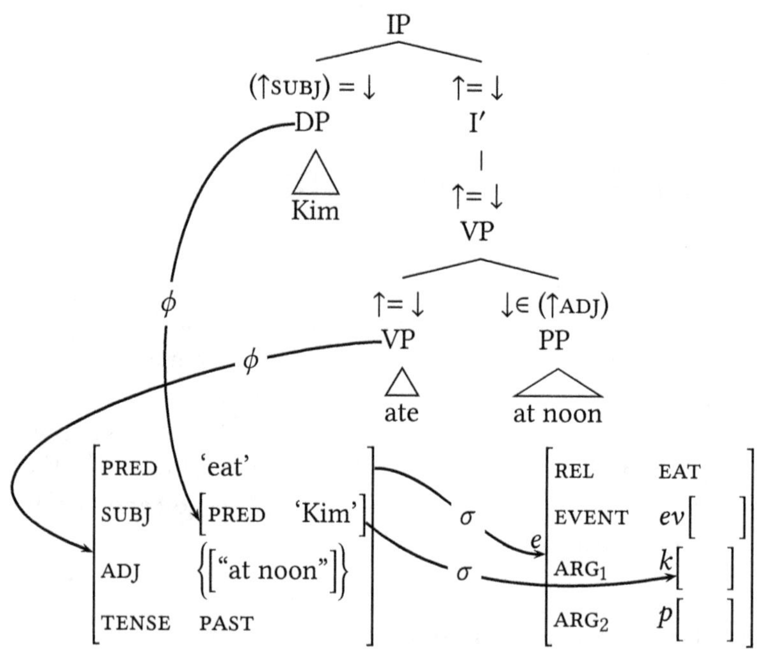

Figure 2.1: Analysis of *Kim ate at noon.* according to Asudeh et al. (2014: 75)

(11) $eat(e) \wedge agent(e) = kim$

Agents and patients are introduced by Findlay's (2016: Section 6.2) templates given in (12):

(12) a. AGENT =
@ARG1
$\lambda P \lambda x \lambda e.P(e) \wedge agent(e) = x :$
$[(\uparrow_\sigma \text{ EVENT}) \multimap \uparrow_\sigma] \multimap (\uparrow_\sigma \text{ ARG}_1) \multimap (\uparrow_\sigma \text{ EVENT}) \multimap \uparrow_\sigma$

b. PATIENT =
@ARG2
$\lambda P \lambda x \lambda e.P(e) \wedge patient(e) = x :$
$[(\uparrow_\sigma \text{ EVENT}) \multimap \uparrow_\sigma] \multimap (\uparrow_\sigma \text{ ARG}_2) \multimap (\uparrow_\sigma \text{ EVENT}) \multimap \uparrow_\sigma$

These templates call further templates called ARG1 and ARG2, respectively, and provide a meaning constructor that consists of a lambda expression (line two) and a glue expression (line three). The lambda expression in both templates is looking for a *P*. This *P* can only be combined with the lambda expression if it simultaneously provides the resource $[(\uparrow_\sigma \text{ EVENT}) \multimap \uparrow_\sigma]$. After the consumption of this resource the formula $(\uparrow_\sigma \textsc{arg}_1) \multimap (\uparrow_\sigma \textsc{event}) \multimap \uparrow_\sigma$ results. This formula states that an ARG$_1$ has to be found. After combination with ARG$_1$, the resource $(\uparrow_\sigma \textsc{event}) \multimap \uparrow_\sigma$ can be consumed by a tense predicate resulting in $\uparrow_\sigma$. That is, we arrive at a complete semantic proof that has used all resources. The actual proof involving the templates in (12) is given in Figure 2.2 on page 17 and will be discussed in more detail below.

The templates ARG1 and ARG2 are defined as shown in (13a) and (13b), respectively. For completeness, I also give the definitions of ARG3 and ARG4.

(13) a. ARG1 =
{ @MAP(MINUSO,ARG$_1$) | @NOMAP(ARG$_1$) }

b. ARG2 =
{ @MAP(MINUSR,ARG$_2$) | @NOMAP(ARG$_2$) }

c. ARG3 =
{ @MAP(PLUSO,ARG$_3$) | @NOMAP(ARG$_3$) }

d. ARG4 =
{ @MAP(MINUSO,ARG$_4$) | @NOMAP(ARG$_4$) }

The templates MAP and NOMAP are used in (13) to either map the arguments to a disjunction of grammatical functions or to declare that they are not mapped to f-structure items at all. The disjunctions of grammatical functions correspond to disjunctions that are assumed in Lexical Mapping Theory and are given in (14):[1]

(14) a. MINUSR ≡ {SUBJ|OBJ} $[-r]$

b. MINUSO ≡ {SUBJ|OBL$_\theta$} $[-o]$

c. PLUSR ≡ {OBL$_\theta$|OBJ$_\theta$} $[+r]$

d. PLUSO ≡ {OBJ|OBJ$_\theta$} $[+o]$

The templates MAP and NOMAP are defined as follows:

(15) a. MAP(F,A) =
$(\uparrow \text{F})_\sigma = (\uparrow_\sigma \text{A})$

b. NOMAP(A) =
$(\uparrow_\sigma \text{A})_{\sigma^{-1}} = \varnothing$

The template MAP takes its first argument F and states that the value of the σ function of the value of F in the f-structure of the mother equals the A value in the σ structure of the mother.

[1] PLUSR is not used anywhere in this book, but it plays a role in the analysis of the passive (Findlay 2016: 319; Asudeh et al. 2014: 78).

The template NoMap says that the element A in a σ structure is not mapped to a grammatical function in the f-structure that belongs to the A feature (identified via an inverse function from the semantic structure to the f-structure (σ^{-1})).

If we expand the templates for Arg1, Arg2, and Arg3, we get:

(16) a. Arg1 =
$\{ (\uparrow\{\text{SUBJ}|\text{OBL}_\theta\})_\sigma = (\uparrow_\sigma \text{ARG}_1) \mid (\uparrow_\sigma \text{ARG}_1)_{\sigma^{-1}} = \varnothing \}$

b. Arg2 =
$\{ (\uparrow\{\text{SUBJ}|\text{OBJ}\})_\sigma = (\uparrow_\sigma \text{ARG}_2) \mid (\uparrow_\sigma \text{ARG}_2)_{\sigma^{-1}} = \varnothing \}$

c. Arg3 =
$\{ (\uparrow\{\text{OBJ}|\text{OBJ}_\theta\})_\sigma = (\uparrow_\sigma \text{ARG}_3) \mid (\uparrow_\sigma \text{ARG}_3)_{\sigma^{-1}} = \varnothing \}$

(16a) says that either the σ value of the subj is ARG_1 or the σ value of the OBL_θ is ARG_1 or ARG_1 is not realized in the f-structure at all. (16b) says that ARG_2 is mapped to subj or obj or to nothing at all and (16c) says that ARG_3 is mapped to obj or OBJ_θ or to nothing at all.

For verbs like *draw*, which have both an agent and a patient, the templates for agent and patient can be combined into one template as in (17):

(17) Agent-Patient =
@Agent
@Patient

Finally we need the template Past in (18):

(18) Past =
$(\uparrow \text{TENSE}) = \text{PAST}$
$\lambda P \exists e.[P(e) \wedge past(e)]$:
$[(\uparrow_\sigma \text{EVENT}) \multimap \uparrow_\sigma] \multimap \uparrow_\sigma$

This template adds the tense feature and the value past to the f-structure, adds the past semantics to an event and states a glue term that requires something that takes an event and licenses a complete σ structure$[(\uparrow_\sigma \text{EVENT}) \multimap \uparrow_\sigma]$. If this resource is found, a complete σ structure $\uparrow_\sigma$ results.

With the template for Past in place, we can now have a look at the lexical entry for *drew* in (19):

(19) *drew* V
$(\uparrow \text{PRED}) = \text{‘draw’}$
@Past
@Agent-Patient
$\lambda e.draw(e) : (\uparrow_\sigma \text{EVENT}) \multimap \uparrow_\sigma$

The specification of the PRED value in (19) is unusual for LFG. Usually, PRED values come with a specification of grammatical functions that have to be realized together with a predicate. The PRED value is the representation of valence information in LFG. This function is taken over by glue terms in proposals that use glue semantics. Since glue semantics is resource sensitive, one can set things up in a way to make sure that all the grammatical functions that are required to fill semantic roles are realized in an utterance.

If we expand the template calls, we get the f-structure constraints and semantic constructors in (20):

(20) *drew* V
$(\uparrow \text{PRED}) = \text{`draw'}$
$(\uparrow \text{TENSE}) = \text{PAST}$
$\{ (\uparrow\{\text{SUBJ}|\text{OBL}_\theta\})_\sigma = (\uparrow_\sigma \text{ARG}_1) \mid (\uparrow_\sigma \text{ARG}_1)_{\sigma^{-1}} = \varnothing \}$
$\{ (\uparrow\{\text{SUBJ}|\text{OBJ}\})_\sigma = (\uparrow_\sigma \text{ARG}_2) \mid (\uparrow_\sigma \text{ARG}_2)_{\sigma^{-1}} = \varnothing \}$
$\lambda P \exists e.[P(e) \wedge past(e)]:$
$[(\uparrow_\sigma \text{EVENT}) \multimap \uparrow_\sigma] \multimap \uparrow_\sigma$
$\lambda P \lambda x \lambda e.P(e) \wedge agent(e) = x:$
$[(\uparrow_\sigma \text{EVENT}) \multimap \uparrow_\sigma] \multimap (\uparrow_\sigma \text{ARG}_1) \multimap (\uparrow_\sigma \text{EVENT}) \multimap \uparrow_\sigma$
$\lambda P \lambda x \lambda e.P(e) \wedge patient(e) = x:$
$[(\uparrow_\sigma \text{EVENT}) \multimap \uparrow_\sigma] \multimap (\uparrow_\sigma \text{ARG}_2) \multimap (\uparrow_\sigma \text{EVENT}) \multimap \uparrow_\sigma$
$\lambda e.draw(e) : (\uparrow_\sigma \text{EVENT}) \multimap \uparrow_\sigma$

The glue terms can be used in a proof as is shown in the box for *draw′* in Figure 2.2 on page 17. The proofs are basically lambda reductions with the additional condition that resources that are paired with the lambda expression (the material to the right of the colon) have to be used. So, for instance, when @PATIENT is combined with *drew*, the resource (ev ⊸ d) ⊸ s ⊸ ev ⊸ d has to be used. Since *drew* provides ev ⊸ d, the combination of the two items results in s ⊸ ev ⊸ d. In the next step, an x:s is hypothesized, lambda reduction takes place and the resource s is consumed yielding ev ⊸ d. This expression is combined with @AGENT. @AGENT contains the glue term (ev ⊸ d) ⊸ k ⊸ ev ⊸ d and since @PATIENT + *drew* was ev ⊸ d, a combination is possible and the result is k ⊸ ev ⊸ d. Now the x:s that was hypothesized earlier is reintroduced into the formula resulting in s ⊸ k ⊸ ev ⊸ d.

Asudeh, Giorgolo & Toivonen (2014: 81) assume that information about benefactive arguments is introduced by the c-structure rule in (21):

(21) $\text{V}' \rightarrow \underset{(\,@\text{BENEFACTIVE}\,)}{\overset{\text{V}}{\uparrow = \downarrow}} \quad \overset{\text{DP}}{(\uparrow \text{OBJ}) = \downarrow} \quad \overset{\text{DP}}{(\uparrow \text{OBJ}_\theta) = \downarrow}$

The BENEFACTIVE template is specified in brackets, which – in the context of template calls – marks optionality. So the c-structure rule can be used with normal ditransitive verbs or with transitive verbs and, in this case, the BENEFACTIVE template would apply and license a further argument.

The BENEFACTIVE template is defined as follows:

(22) BENEFACTIVE =
@ARG3
$\lambda x \lambda y \lambda P \lambda e.P(y)(e) \wedge \mathit{beneficiary}(e) = x$:
$(\uparrow_\sigma \text{ARG}_2) \multimap (\uparrow_\sigma \text{ARG}_3) \multimap [(\uparrow_\sigma \text{ARG}_2) \multimap (\uparrow_\sigma \text{EVENT}) \multimap \uparrow_\sigma] \multimap (\uparrow_\sigma \text{EVENT}) \multimap \uparrow_\sigma$

As Asudeh et al. (2014: 78) state, the template uses a trick. It first looks for ARG_2 and ARG_3 and then combines with a verb looking for an ARG_2. In this way the resource logic basically maps a two-place predicate to a three-place predicate.

If we expand the call to the ARG3 template, we get (23):

(23) $\{ (\uparrow\{\text{OBJ}|\text{OBJ}_\theta\})_\sigma = (\uparrow_\sigma \text{ARG}_3) \mid (\uparrow_\sigma \text{ARG}_3)_{\sigma^{-1}} = \varnothing \}$
$\lambda x \lambda y \lambda P \lambda e.P(y)(e) \wedge \mathit{beneficiary}(e) = x$:
$(\uparrow_\sigma \text{ARG}_2) \multimap (\uparrow_\sigma \text{ARG}_3) \multimap [(\uparrow_\sigma \text{ARG}_2) \multimap (\uparrow_\sigma \text{EVENT}) \multimap \uparrow_\sigma] \multimap (\uparrow_\sigma \text{EVENT}) \multimap \uparrow_\sigma$

In an analysis of (24), we would hence have the constraints on the lexical item for *drew* given in (19) and the constraints in (23).

(24) Kim drew Sandy Godzilla.

This means that the grammatical functions of the arguments are underspecified in the c-structure annotations of the lexical item and the benefactive template. What we have so far is the set of constraints given in (16). In order to get these disjunctions resolved, we need c-structure rules. In the case at hand we have the c-structure rule in (21) that licenses the objects and we have an IP rule that combines the VP with an NP/DP. This c-structure rule ensures that there is a SUBJ. Without these additional constraints from c-structure configurations, the approach would overgenerate. As I will show in Chapter 5, this is problematic since the assignment of grammatical functions in passives has to be taken care of by c-structure rules that are specific to the benefactive construction, which results in missing generalizations.

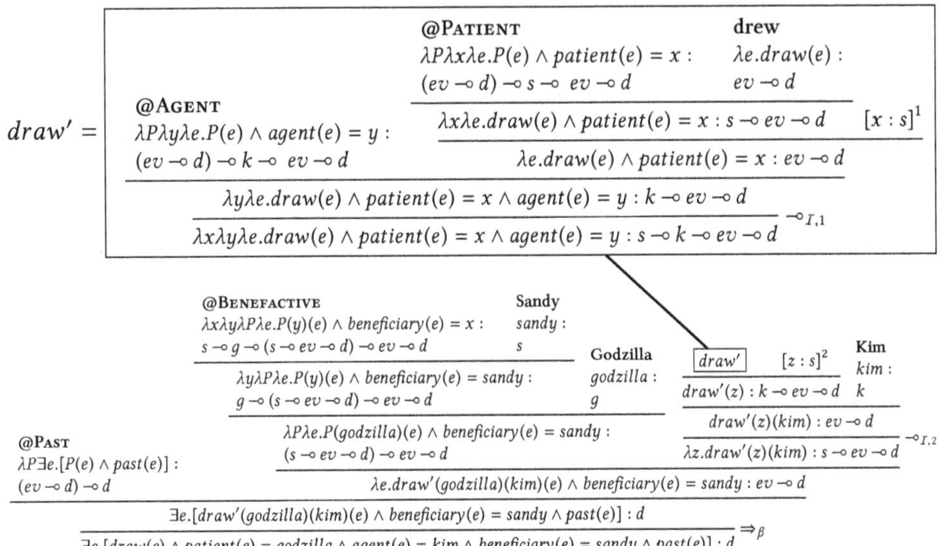

Figure 2.2: Proof for *Kim drew Sandy Godzilla.*

2.1.2 Inheritance-based analyses: Why do they work and where are the limits

Müller (2010b) argued that semantics needs embedding and cannot be done in inheritance networks. For instance, it was suggested to do morphology by inheritance. As Krieger & Nerbonne (1993) show this fails for adjectives like *undoable*. *undoable* has two possible meanings that correspond to two bracketings: *undo-able* and *un-doable*. In the first reading, the verb *undo* is combined with *-able*; the verbal meaning is embedded under a modal operator. In the second reading, the prefix *un-* is attached to the adjective *doable* and embeds the meaning of *doable* under the negation. If semantic information is the value of a feature and if the properties of *undoable* are inherited from *un-*, *do*, and *-able*, we get a conflict because rather than inheriting three incompatible semantic contributions from the verb and the affixes, the contribution of the verb has to be embedded under the contribution of one of the affixes and the result has to be embedded under the contribution of the other affix.

Müller (2007a), Müller (2013b) and Müller & Wechsler (2014a) argued that argument structure changing phenomena cannot be treated via inheritance but need formal means that map representations to other representations. An example for such problems are causative constructions in languages like Turkish. Such causative constructions license additional arguments and they can be iterated.

The analysis of Asudeh et al. (2014) seems to falsify my claims and seems to suggest that there is a way to analyze argument structure constructions phrasally with inheritance of constraints playing an important role.

Traditional a-structure-based LFG approaches assume that sentences with different argument realizations have different lexical items with different argument structure representations. The argument structures are mapped to grammatical functions and these are realized according to the syntax of the respective languages. For instance, Bresnan et al. (2015: Section 14.4.5) assume the following a-structures for the transitive and the ditransitive use of *cook*:

(25) a. Transitive:

a-structure:	*cook*	⟨	agent	patient	⟩
			[−o]	[−r]	
f-structure:			SUBJ	OBJ	

b. Ditransitive:

a-structure:	*cook-for*	⟨	agent	beneficiary	patient	⟩
			[−o]	[−r]	[+o]	
f-structure:			SUBJ	OBJ	OBJ_θ	

Lexical Mapping Theory makes sure that the arguments that are labeled with −o, −r and +o are mapped to the respective grammatical functions. The important point about this analysis is that there are two lexemes: one for transitive *cook* with an a-structure that contains two elements and one for the ditransitive version with an a-structure that contains three elements. The a-structures are ordered lists with a fixed arity and it is impossible to add an element into the middle of such a list by a monotonic gathering of constraints (e.g., inheritance).[2] The template-based approach circumvents this problem by not stipulating an order of elements in a list. Rather than using an ordered representation like lists, it assumes an s-structure into which features can be added by simple unification. These features are not ordered. The feature names have numbers as part of the names but this is just mnemonic and if order effects are desired they have to be modeled elsewhere. Asudeh et al. (2014) impose the order-specific constraints in the glue part of their semantic expressions. For instance, the BENEFACTIVE template refers to ARG_2 and ARG_3 and consumes respective resources in a specified order.

[2] It is possible to extend lists at the end if defaults and overriding are permitted. See Müller (2017b) for discussion. It is also possible to leave the number of elements in a list underspecified and state constraints on membership and order in such lists. See Müller (2007a: Section 7.5.2) for problems of such accounts.

Turning to semantics, the claims regarding inheritance and embedding are true for frameworks in which the semantic contribution is represented as a value of a feature (HPSG, Pollard & Sag 1994; Sag 1997; BCG, Kay & Fillmore 1999; SBCG, Sag 2012; FCG, Steels 2011). If two different semantic values are inherited from supertypes, a conflict arises. To take an example, consider the Agent and the Patient template. If we assumed that the meaning-constructor is the value of a feature, say sem, we would have two conflicting values:

(26) a. $\lambda P \lambda x \lambda e.P(e) \wedge agent(e) = x :$
$[(\uparrow_\sigma \textsc{event}) \multimap \uparrow_\sigma] \multimap (\uparrow_\sigma \textsc{arg}_1) \multimap (\uparrow_\sigma \textsc{event}) \multimap \uparrow_\sigma$

b. $\lambda P \lambda x \lambda e.P(e) \wedge patient(e) = x :$
$[(\uparrow_\sigma \textsc{event}) \multimap \uparrow_\sigma] \multimap (\uparrow_\sigma \textsc{arg}_2) \multimap (\uparrow_\sigma \textsc{event}) \multimap \uparrow_\sigma$

Note that representing these semantic contributions in lists would not help either, since this would just shift the conflict to another place. Lists are ordered and if (26a) is the first member of a list and (26b) is the first member of a second list, the two lists are incompatible. In order to avoid such conflicts auxiliary features and mappings between auxiliary features may be used (Koenig 1999). The problem is that one auxiliary feature per interaction is needed (Müller 2007a: Section 7.5.2.2).

Assuming sets rather than lists would not work either, if the general understanding of sets as is common in HPSG (Pollard & Moshier 1990) is assumed. What could be done is that one inherits constraints on list or set membership. The Agent and Patient templates would then have the following feature-value specification:

(27) a. $\textsc{sem}\ \boxed{1} \wedge \lambda P \lambda x \lambda e.P(e) \wedge agent(e) = x : \quad \in \boxed{1}$
$[(\uparrow_\sigma \textsc{event}) \multimap \uparrow_\sigma] \multimap (\uparrow_\sigma \textsc{arg}_1) \multimap (\uparrow_\sigma \textsc{event}) \multimap \uparrow_\sigma$

b. $\textsc{sem}\ \boxed{1} \wedge \lambda P \lambda x \lambda e.P(e) \wedge patient(e) = x : \quad \in \boxed{1}$
$[(\uparrow_\sigma \textsc{event}) \multimap \uparrow_\sigma] \multimap (\uparrow_\sigma \textsc{arg}_2) \multimap (\uparrow_\sigma \textsc{event}) \multimap \uparrow_\sigma$

So one would say that the value of sem is a set ($\boxed{1}$) and that the meaning constructor for agent is an element of this set and that the meaning constructor for patient is an element of this set too. Note that the set is not constrained otherwise, in principle any formula could be part of this set. So one would need the additional assumption that we are looking for minimal models when we interpret linguistic structures, an assumption that is usually made in LFG.

In general, such a system of semantics construction would not work since it would not be clear in which order partial formulae that are inherited from supertypes are to be combined. Authors have used semantic types in order to make it clear what type of argument has to be combined with a certain functor (e.g., in GPSG, Gazdar et al. 1985: Chapters 9–10), but this does not help in all cases. The glue approach has additional means to specify what is combined with what: specific resources are used when elements are combined. So, while the lambda expressions for the agent and the patient template in (27) are identical, the glue resources are not. The AGENT template involves an $\textsc{arg}_1$ and the PATIENT template an $\textsc{arg}_2$. Furthermore, the glue apparatus can be used for mapping predicates of a certain arity to predicates of another arity. For instance, the BENEFACTIVE template requires an $\textsc{arg}_2$ and an $\textsc{arg}_3$ and then a verb that selects for an $\textsc{arg}_2$ ($[(\uparrow_\sigma \textsc{arg}_2) \multimap (\uparrow_\sigma \textsc{event}) \multimap \uparrow_\sigma]$).

(28) Part of the BENEFACTIVE template that remaps $\textsc{arg}_2$ to $\textsc{arg}_3$:
$(\uparrow_\sigma \textsc{arg}_2) \multimap (\uparrow_\sigma \textsc{arg}_3) \multimap [(\uparrow_\sigma \textsc{arg}_2) \multimap (\uparrow_\sigma \textsc{event}) \multimap \uparrow_\sigma]$

This basically turns a two-place verb selecting for an object ($\textsc{arg}_2$) into a three-place verb that has a new first object ($\textsc{arg}_2$) and realizes the object of the two-place verb as its second object ($\textsc{arg}_3$). The glue term basically does what a lexical rule does in lexical rule-based systems, it maps a two-place predicate to a three-place predicate:

(29) $\left\langle \textsc{arg}_x, \textsc{arg}_y \right\rangle \mapsto \left\langle \textsc{arg}_x, \textsc{arg}_z, \textsc{arg}_y \right\rangle$

So a lexical item with several glue constraints attached to it corresponds to a lexical item with several lexical rules attached to it (for later application). The resource sensitivity of the glue statements ensures that the glue statements are used in a specific order in the proofs. Similarly, the input and output conditions of lexical rules make sure that they are applied in a certain order.[3]

2.2 Resultative constructions

Christie (2010) assumes the c-structure rule in (31) for transitive resultative constructions like the one in (30):

(30) He hammered the metal flat.

[3] See, for instance, Blevins (2003: 515) for the application of the impersonal lexical rule to the output of the passivization lexical rule. The output of the impersonal lexical rule cannot function as input to passivization since passivization requires a subject to be suppressed and the subject was already suppressed by the impersonalization.

(31) $$\begin{array}{llccc} \text{V}' & \rightarrow & \text{V} & \text{DP} & \{\,\text{DP}|\text{AP}|\text{PP}\,\} \\ & & \uparrow = \downarrow & (\uparrow \textsc{obj}) = \downarrow & (\uparrow \textsc{xcomp}) = \downarrow \\ & & & & (\downarrow \textsc{subj}) = (\uparrow \textsc{obj}) \\ & & & & @\textsc{result-t}((\uparrow \textsc{pred fn})) \end{array}$$

The resultative template licenses the result predicate and provides a glue semantics term that licenses subject and object. Christie (2010) assumes the following lexical entry for the transitive verb *hammer*:

(32) hammer V $\lambda e.hammer(e) : (\uparrow_\sigma \textsc{rel})$
$$\left(\begin{array}{l} @\textsc{transitive}(\text{hammer}) \\ \lambda P \lambda x \lambda y \lambda e.P(e) \wedge agent(e) = x \wedge patient(e) = y\text{:} \\ (\uparrow_\sigma \textsc{rel}) \multimap (\uparrow \textsc{subj})_\sigma \multimap (\uparrow \textsc{obj})_\sigma \multimap \uparrow_\sigma \end{array}\right)$$

The resource sensitive semantics and the specification of a PRED value is declared to be optional. When these verbs are used in the c-structure rule in (31), the lexical information is replaced by the information contributed by the resultative template. Christie assumes that all sentences must have a specified PRED value and therefore the optional PRED value must be realized in simple sentences without a result predicate.

Christie does not explain how resultatives with intransitive verbs as in (5), repeated here as (33) for convenience, are analyzed but by analogy there would be lexical items for intransitive verbs with an optional meaning contribution and a resultative template which integrates the meaning of the result predicate with the meaning of the intransitive verb, and which licenses an additional object argument.

(33) He runs his sneakers threadbare.

The previous subsections introduced the phrasal template-based analyses of benefactive constructions and resultative constructions by Asudeh et al. (2014) and Christie (2010). In what follows, I will explain the problematic aspects. I start with a section that shows that neither the resultative construction nor the benefactive construction is fixed in its form. The data challenges Toivonen's motivations for a phrasal construction (Toivonen 2013).

3 The flexibility of the constructions

Christie (2010), Toivonen (2013) and Asudeh et al. (2014) suggest phrasal constructions for resultative and benefactive constructions with a fixed number of daughters on the right-hand side of the c-structure rule. Christie (2010) proposes the following c-structure rule for the introduction of the result predicate and its subject:

(34) V′ →

V	DP	{ DP|AP|PP }
↑ = ↓	(↑ OBJ) = ↓	(↑ XCOMP) = ↓
		(↓ SUBJ) = (↑ OBJ)
		@RESULT-T((↑PRED FN))

In Christie's analysis, verbs are assumed to only optionally provide semantic and f-structure constraints. If they enter the resultative construction in (34), the construction takes over and provides a PRED value and specifications for grammatical functions.

The rule for the benefactive construction in (35) was provided in (21) and is repeated here as (36) for convenience:

(35) The performer sang the children a song.

(36) V′ →

V	DP	DP
↑ = ↓	(↑ OBJ) = ↓	(↑ OBJ_θ) = ↓
(@BENEFACTIVE)		

According to the Asudeh et al. (2014: 81), the noun phrase *the children* is not an argument of *sing* but is contributed by the c-structure rule that optionally licenses a benefactive.

As will be shown in the following, neither the resultative construction nor the benefactive construction is fixed in this form. Let us look at resultatives first. Carrier & Randall (1992: 185) discuss extraction data like those in (37):

(37) a. ? How shiny do you wonder which gems to polish?

b. ? Which colors do you wonder which shirts to dye?

These examples show that it is possible to extract both the result phrase and the object. As we see in the examples in (38), the objects can be extracted with the result predicate remaining in the V′:

(38) a. I wonder which gems to polish shiny.
 b. I wonder which shirts to dye that color.

It is also possible to extract the result predicate and leave the object in place:

(39) a. I wonder how shiny to polish the gems.
 b. I wonder which color to dye the shirts.

Apart from extraction, passivization is possible as well:

(40) a. The shoes were polished shiny.
 b. The shirts were dyed a different color.

This means that the object, the result predicate, or both the object and the result predicate may be missing from the resultative construction in (34). The same is true for the benefactive construction. Asudeh et al. (2014) deal with grammars of speakers of English that allow for passivization of benefactive constructions. For those speakers all examples in (41) are fine:

(41) a. Her husband prepared her divine and elaborate meals.
 b. She had been prepared divine and elaborate meals.
 c. Such divine and elaborate meals, she had never been prepared before, not even by her ex-husband who was a professional chef.

The examples show that some speakers permit the promotion of the benefactive to subject as in (41b,c) and the remaining object can be extracted as in (41c).

While the extraction of the benefactive is out as (7d), repeated here as (42a), shows, the examples in (42b,c) show that the secondary object in a benefactive construction can be extracted.

(42) a. * Which teacher did the kids draw a picture?
 b. What kind of picture did the kids draw the teacher?
 c. the picture that the kids drew the teacher

The benefactives seem to pattern with normal ditransitives here. For an overview, citing several other sources, see Hudson (1992: 258). Hudson reports that the extraction of the primary object of normal ditransitives is also judged as marked or even ungrammatical by many authors and informants:

(43) a. We give children sweets.
 b. Which sweets do you give children _?
 c. % Which children do you give _ sweets?

Some variants of LFG account for extraction by assuming that the extracted element is not realized locally. The respective daughter in a rule is optional and the place in the f-structure is filled via functional uncertainty (Kaplan & Zaenen 1989; Dalrymple 2001: 415; Dalrymple, Kaplan & King 2001; Zaenen & Kaplan 2002). This means that in (37) and (41c), we have a situation in which it is just the verb that remains in the VP. All other elements are either promoted to grammatical functions that are realized outside of the VP or they are extracted. Thus nothing is left of the original configuration, it is just the verb. Christie's (2010) analysis of the resultative would be in deep trouble since she assumed that the resultative template is optionally introduced at the result predicate and overwrites optional information coming from the verb. As is clear from looking at the examples in (37), attaching the constraint to the extracted result predicate would be inappropriate since the result predicate can be fronted and would appear in another local domain (the one of *wonder* rather than *dye*, compare also the discussion of (68)). The constraints would apply to the wrong f-structure. The phrasal approach could be saved by assuming traces (as Berman (2003: Chapter 6) does for extraction crossing clause boundaries). This would be compatible with Christie's proposal since the structure would remain the same with some arguments being realized by empty elements.[1]

The situation with the benefactive construction is similar: in (41c) we have a bare verb and all other items are promoted or extracted. The template is associated with the verb. One could either insist on the phrasal pattern in (21) and posit an additional rule for the passive (see Chapter 5) and a trace for extraction or assume that constituents are optional and that rules like (21) can be used

[1]Mary Dalrymple and Miriam Butt (p. c. 2016) pointed out another solution to me: one can annotate the c-structure rule for the CP that combines an extracted phrase and a C′. Extracted phrases find the place in the f-structure that belongs to the place from which they are extracted by functional uncertainty. The resultative template could be associated with the respective place in the f-structure by functional uncertainty as well. However, we would then have a grammar that introduces resultative constructions in at least two places: SpecCP and in a special resultative V′. A generalization about English (and German) is that constituents can be extracted out of their local contexts and be fronted. Although technically possible, I consider it inappropriate to state at the SpecCP node any information about the internal structure of subconstituents from which the extraction took place. For certain types of resultative constructions, a resultative template in fronted position would license an additional object and result predicate in an embedded V′. Note also that authors who assume a phrasal resultative construction would probably also want to assume other phrasal constructions as well. If these allow extraction of crucial parts, the respective annotations at SpecCP would be necessary. The generalization about extraction would be missed. (See also the discussion of Figure 6.4 below.)

In addition, the lexical approach assumes one place where the resultative predicate is licensed: the lexical rule. The phrasal approach would assume at least two (unrelated) places. On Occamian grounds, the lexical analysis is to be preferred.

to account for all examples in (41). Under the latter proposal, the c-structure is not really restrictive. In the analysis of (41c), only the verb is present and one therefore could assume a lexical approach in which the benefactive template is associated with the verb right away. (See the discussion of (58), which suggests that there is an advantage for the lexical proposal.)

Asudeh et al. (2014: 81) state that "The call to BENEFACTIVE is optional, such that the double-object rule is general and can also apply to non-benefactive cases." If passivization and extraction are treated by declaring arguments to be optional, this also has to be reflected in the phrase structure rule in (21). The rule has to account for both verbs with a benefactive argument and normal ditransitive verbs. If the rule in (21) is supposed to rule out passives like (8), repeated here as (44) for convenience, the benefactive NP has to be obligatory.

(44) * My sister was carved a soap statue of Bugs Bunny (by a famous sculptor).

However, this would also rule out passives of normal ditransitives like (45).

(45) My sister was given a soap statue of Bugs Bunny (by a famous sculptor).

So, if the rule were responsible for normal ditransitives as well as for benefactives, all constraints regarding the obligatory presence of daughters would have to reside in the template since this is the only part that is different between benefactives and normal ditransitives. The templates defined by Asudeh et al. (2014) contain semantic constraints and constraints relevant for argument structure mappings. Nothing syntactic is encoded there. So, either the authors assume that benefactives pattern like normal ditransitives syntactically in the speaker group that they examine and then there would be no need to introduce the benefactive argument phrasally or there is a difference and then a special benefactive c-structure rule should be assumed that is incompatible with normal ditransitive verbs.[2]

[2] An alternative may be to say that the V′ rule with two objects is for benefactives and for ditransitive verbs with all objects realized in the VP. One would then assume that the passive of ditransitives is taken care of by the phrase structure rule in (i).

(i) V′ → V DP
$\uparrow = \downarrow$ $(\uparrow \text{OBJ}_\theta) = \downarrow$

Since the benefactive template is not mentioned in this rule, no benefactive argument would be licensed in the respective configuration. Bresnan, Asudeh, Toivonen & Wechsler (2015) state that OBJ_θ is the grammatical function for secondary objects. Hence, a rule like (i) is a special rule with a missing primary object. The only purpose (i) would serve in a grammar of English would be to account for the passive and primary object extraction of ditransitive verbs. The rule would be a stipulation and a generalization about the passivizability of ditransitive verbs would be missed.

Before I turn to the analysis of active/passive alternations, I want to take a look at the interaction of morphology and the constructions under consideration.

4 Morphology and valence

Morphological processes have to be able to see the valence of the element they apply to (this point was also made by Müller & Wechsler (2014a: Section 4.2) in connection with the GPSG representation of valence). For instance, the generalization about productive *-bar* 'able' derivation in German is that it only applies to verbs that govern a subject and an accusative object. While *lösbar* 'solvable' and *vergleichbar* 'comparable' can be formed, * *schlafbar* 'sleepable' and * *helfbar* 'helpable' are ruled out:

(46) a. lösbar (NP[nom], NP[acc])
solveable

b. vergleichbar (NP[nom], NP[acc], PP[mit])
comparable

c. * schlafbar (NP[nom])
sleepable

d. * helfbar (NP[nom], NP[dat])
helpable

The resultative construction also interacts with *-bar* 'able' derivation: the adjectives *leerfischbar* 'empty.fish.able' = 'It is possible to fish X empty.' and *plattfahrbar*[1] 'flat.drive.able' can be formed. If arguments are introduced by phrasal configurations which refer to fully derived and inflected words or phrases consisting of words, the accessibility of the valence information to the morphology component is not given and it remains an open question how phrasal analyses can explain the contrasts in (46) and the fact that *-bar* 'able' derivation does apply to verbs in the resultative construction. In Christie's (2010) analysis, the intransitive verbs would probably be represented as intransitive in the lexicon with an optional semantic representation. As was argued in Müller (2003), the derivational affix attaches to the verbal stem and hence the information about an accusative object would not be available in Christie's approach. Even if one assumes that *leer* and *fisch* are combined before the attachment of *-bar*, it is unclear what licenses this combination. The fact that *leerfisch* takes an accusative

[1] http://www.forum-3dcenter.org/vbulletin/archive/index.php/t-236032.htmls, 2016-06-02.

object would have to be available at the point when *-bar* attaches and could not be contributed by phrase structure rules in the syntax. Reviewers suggested that special rules could combine adjectives and verbs in the morphology component and license the object there. While this is possible in principle, this would be an instance of a missed generalization since one would have to assume two unrelated rules that mention the resultative template.

Furthermore, there are resultative constructions with phrasal result phrases like (47) and here it could not be argued that PP and verbal stem form a new verbal stem to which *-bar* attaches.

(47) Die Mauer ist in kleine Stücke fahrbar.
the wall is into small pieces driveable
'The wall can be driven into small pieces.'

If one is ready to follow Bruening (2018) and get rid of the assumption of Lexical Integrity, then (47) can be analyzed as a combination of *in kleine Stücke fahr-* and *-bar*, but if one wants to maintain the view that words are the atoms of syntax (Asudeh et al. 2013: 10), the *-bar* 'able' derivation constitutes evidence against Alsina's and Christie's phrasal approach (as a general approach that also holds for German).

Another example of derivational morphology showing that information about valence is needed at the word level is the derivation of adjectival participles: this derivation is only possible if the verb requires an accusative object. So, when the adjectival participle is derived, this information has to be accessible. Alsina (1996) showed that the passive of resultatives can be accounted for lexically since the subject that has to be suppressed is available in the stem. It can be suppressed when the participle is formed and when further arguments are added in the syntax, these have to be realized as subjects. However, this fails in the case of adjectival participles. The adjective derivation applies to a passivized verbal stem that has at least one argument slot open: the accusative object in the active. (48) shows an example:

(48) a. Er tanzt die Schuhe blutig / in Stücke.
he.NOM dances the.ACC shoes bloody into pieces

b. die in Stücke / blutig getanzten Schuhe
the into pieces bloody danced shoes

c. * die getanzten Schuhe
the danced shoes

The shoes are not a semantic argument of *tanzt*. Nevertheless, the referent of the NP that is realized as accusative NP in (48a) is the element the adjectival participle in (48b) predicates over. Adjectival participles like the one in (48b) are derived from a passive participle of a verb that governs an accusative object. The example in (48c) shows that the passive participle cannot be formed with unergative intransitive verbs. This should be contrasted with a transitive verb like *lieben* 'to love':

(49) der geliebte Mann
the loved man
'the beloved man'

The transitive verb allows the formation of the adjectival participle and the participle with resultative predicate in (48b) behaves completely parallel.

If the accusative object in resultative constructions is licensed phrasally by configurations like the one in (31), it cannot be explained why the participle *getanzte* can be formed despite the absence of an accusative object in the valence specification of the verb. See the next section for further interactions of resultatives and morphology. The conclusion, which was drawn in the late 70s and early 80s by Dowty (1978: 412) and Bresnan (1982: 21), is that phenomena that feed morphology should be treated lexically. The natural analysis in frameworks like HPSG, CG, CxG, and LFG is therefore a lexical one, for example one that assumes a lexical rule for the licensing of resultative constructions. See Verspoor (1997), Wechsler (1997), Wechsler & Noh (2001), Wunderlich (1992: 45; 1997: 120–126), Kaufmann & Wunderlich (1998), Müller (2002: Chapter 5), Simpson (1983) and Christie (2015) for lexical proposals in some of these frameworks.

I now turn to active/passive alternations and point out that the phrasal approach is missing generalizations.

5 Missing generalizations: Active/passive alternations

In this section, I want to show that Asudeh, Giorgolo & Toivonen's (2014) approach to the phrasal introduction of benefactives either does not need to be stated at the phrasal level since the phrasal construction does not contribute relevant information or that the approach misses generalizations regarding the configurations for active and passive.

(50), taken from Asudeh et al. (2014: 72), provides examples of the benefactive construction in an active and a passive variant:

(50) a. The performer sang the children a song.
b. The children were sung a song.

According to the authors, the noun phrase *the children* is not an argument of *sing* but contributed by the c-structure rule in (21), which optionally licenses a benefactive. The rule is repeated here as (51) for convenience:

(51) $V' \rightarrow \underset{\substack{\uparrow = \downarrow \\ (\text{@BENEFACTIVE})}}{V} \quad \underset{(\uparrow \text{OBJ}) = \downarrow}{DP} \quad \underset{(\uparrow \text{OBJ}_\theta) = \downarrow}{DP}$

Whenever this rule is called, the template BENEFACTIVE can add a benefactive role and the respective semantics, provided this is compatible with the verb that is inserted into the structure. The authors show how the mappings for the passive example in (50b) work, but they do not provide the c-structure rule that licenses such examples. Unless one assumes that arguments in (51) can be optional (see below), one would need a c-structure rule for passive VPs and this rule has to license a benefactive as well.[1] So it would be:

(52) $V' \rightarrow \underset{\substack{\uparrow = \downarrow \\ (\text{@BENEFACTIVE})}}{V[\text{pass}]} \quad \underset{(\uparrow \text{OBJ}_\theta) = \downarrow}{DP}$

[1] See, for instance, Bergen & Chang (2005) and van Trijp (2011) for Construction Grammar analyses that assume active and passive variants of phrasal constructions. See Cappelle (2006) on allostructions in general.

Note that a benefactive cannot be added to just any verb: adding a benefactive to an intransitive verb as in (53a) is out and the passive that would correspond to (53a) is ungrammatical as well, as (53b) shows:

(53) a. * He laughed the children.
b. * The children were laughed.

The benefactive template would account for the ungrammaticality of (53) since it requires an ARG$_2$ to be present, but it would admit the sentences in (54b,c) since *give* with prepositional object has an ARG$_2$ (Kibort 2008: 317).

(54) a. He gave it to Mary.
b. * He gave Peter it to Mary.
c. * Peter was given it to Mary.

give could combine with the *to* PP semantically and would then be equivalent to a transitive verb as far as resources are concerned (looking for an ARG$_1$ and an ARG$_2$). The benefactive template would map the ARG$_2$ to ARG$_3$ and hence (54b) would be licensed. Similar examples can be constructed with other verbs that take prepositional objects, for instance *accuse sb. of something*. Since there are verbs that take a benefactive and a PP object as shown by (55), (54b) cannot be ruled out with reference to non-existing c-structure rules.

(55) I buy him a coat for hundred dollar.

So, if the c-structure is to play a role in argument structure constructions at all, one could not just claim that all c-structure rules optionally introduce a benefactive argument. Therefore there is something special about the two rules in (36) and (52). The problem is that there is no relation between these rules. They are independent statements saying that there can be a benefactive in the active and that there can be one in the passive. This is what Chomsky (1957: 43) criticized in 1957 with respect to simple phrase structure grammar and this was the reason for the introduction of transformations. Bresnan-style LFG captured the generalizations by lexical rules (Bresnan 1978; 1982) and later by lexical rules in combination with Lexical Mapping Theory (Toivonen 2013). But if elements are added outside the lexical representations, the representations where these elements are added have to be related too. One could say that our knowledge about formal tools has changed since 1957. We now can use inheritance hierarchies to capture generalizations. So one can assume a type (or a template) that is the supertype of all those c-structure rules that introduce a benefactive. But since not all rules allow for the introduction of a benefactive element, this basically amounts to saying: c-structure rule A, B, and C allow for the introduction of a benefactive. In comparison, lexical rule-based approaches have one statement introducing the benefactive. The lexical rule states what verbs are appropriate for adding a benefactive and syntactic rules are not affected.

Asudeh (p. c. May 2016) and an anonymous reviewer of HeadLex16 pointed out to me that the rules in (51) and (52) can be generalized over if the arguments in (51) are made optional. (56) shows the rule in (51) with the DPs marked as optional by the brackets enclosing them.

(56) $\begin{array}{lccc} V' \rightarrow & V & (DP) & (DP) \\ & \uparrow = \downarrow & (\uparrow \textsc{obj}) = \downarrow & (\uparrow \textsc{obj}_\theta) = \downarrow \\ & (\ @\textsc{Benefactive}\ ) & & \end{array}$

Since both of the DPs are optional, (56) is equivalent to a specification of four rules, namely (51) and the three versions of the rule in (57):

(57) a. $\begin{array}{lcc} V' \rightarrow & V & DP \\ & \uparrow = \downarrow & (\uparrow \textsc{obj}_\theta) = \downarrow \\ & (\ @\textsc{Benefactive}\ ) & \end{array}$

b. $\begin{array}{lcc} V' \rightarrow & V & DP \\ & \uparrow = \downarrow & (\uparrow \textsc{obj}) = \downarrow \\ & (\ @\textsc{Benefactive}\ ) & \end{array}$

c. $\begin{array}{lc} V' \rightarrow & V \\ & \uparrow = \downarrow \\ & (\ @\textsc{Benefactive}\ ) \end{array}$

(57a) is the variant of (56) in which the OBJ is omitted (needed for (41b)), (57b) is the variant in which the $\textsc{obj}_\theta$ is omitted (needed for (42)) and in (57c) both DPs are omitted (needed for (41c)). Hence, (56) can be used for V′s containing two objects, for V′s in the passive containing just one object, for V′ with the secondary object extracted and for V′ in the passive with the secondary object extracted. The template-based approach does not overgenerate since the benefactive template is specified such that it requires the verb it applies to to select for an $\textsc{arg}_2$. Since intransitives like *laugh* do not select an $\textsc{arg}_2$, a benefactive cannot be added. So, in fact, the actual configuration in the c-structure rule does only play a minor role: the account mainly relies on semantics and resource sensitivity. There is one piece of information that is contributed by the c-structure rule: it constrains the grammatical functions of $\textsc{arg}_2$ and $\textsc{arg}_3$, which are underspecified in the template definitions for $\textsc{arg}_2$ and $\textsc{arg}_3$ (see the discussion on page 16). $\textsc{arg}_2$ can be realized as SUBJ or as OBJ. In the active case, $\textsc{arg}_1$ will be the SUBJ and, because of function argument bi-uniqueness (Bresnan et al. 2015: 334), no other element can be the SUBJ and hence ARG$_2$ has to be an OBJ. ARG$_3$ can be either an OBJ or an OBJ$_\theta$. Since ARG$_2$ is an OBJ in the active, ARG$_3$ has to be an OBJ$_\theta$ in the active. In the passive case, ARG$_1$ is suppressed or realized as OBL$_\theta$ (*by* PP). ARG$_2$ will be realized as SUBJ (since English requires a SUBJ to be realized) and ARG$_3$ could be realized as either OBJ or OBJ$_\theta$. This is not constrained by the template specifications so far. Because of the optionality in (56), either the OBJ or the OBJ$_\theta$ function could be chosen for ARG$_3$. This means that either Lexical Mapping Theory has to be revised or one has to make sure that the c-structure rule used in the passive of benefactives states the grammatical function of the object correctly. Hence one would need the c-structure rule in (52) and then there would be the missing generalization I pointed out above.

If one finds a way to set up the mappings to grammatical functions without reference to c-structures in lexical templates, this means that it is not the case that an argument is added by a certain configuration the verb enters in. Since any verb may enter (57) and since the only important thing is the interaction between the lexical specification of the verb and the benefactive template, the same structures would be licensed if the benefactive template were added to the lexical items of verbs directly. The actual configuration would not constrain anything. All (alleged) arguments from language acquisition and psycholinguistics (for an overview of such arguments see Müller & Wechsler (2014a,b)) for phrasal analyses would not apply to such a phrasal account.

If the actual c-structure configuration does not contribute any restrictions as to what arguments may be realized and what grammatical functions they get, the difference between the lexical use of the benefactive template and the phrasal introduction as executed in (56) is really minimal. However, there is one area in grammar where there is a difference: coordination. As Müller & Wechsler (2014a: Section 6.1) pointed out, it is possible to coordinate ditransitive verbs with verbs that appear together with a benefactive. (58) is one of their examples:

(58) She then offered and made me a wonderful espresso – nice.[2]

If the benefactive information is introduced at the lexical level, the coordinated verbs basically have the same selectional requirements. If the benefactive information is introduced at the phrasal level, *baked* and *gave* are coordinated and then the benefactive constraints are imposed on the result of the coordination by the c-structure rule. While it is clear that the lexical items that would be assumed in a lexical approach can be coordinated in a symmetric coordination,

[2] http://www.thespinroom.com.au/?p=102, 2012-07-07.

problems seem to arise for the phrasal approach. It is unclear how the asymmetric coordination of the mono- and ditransitive verbs can be accounted for and how the constraints of the benefactive template are distributed over the two conjuncts. The fact that the benefactive template is optional does not help here since the optionality means that the template is either called or it is not. The situation is depicted in Figure 5.1. The optionality of the template call in the top figure

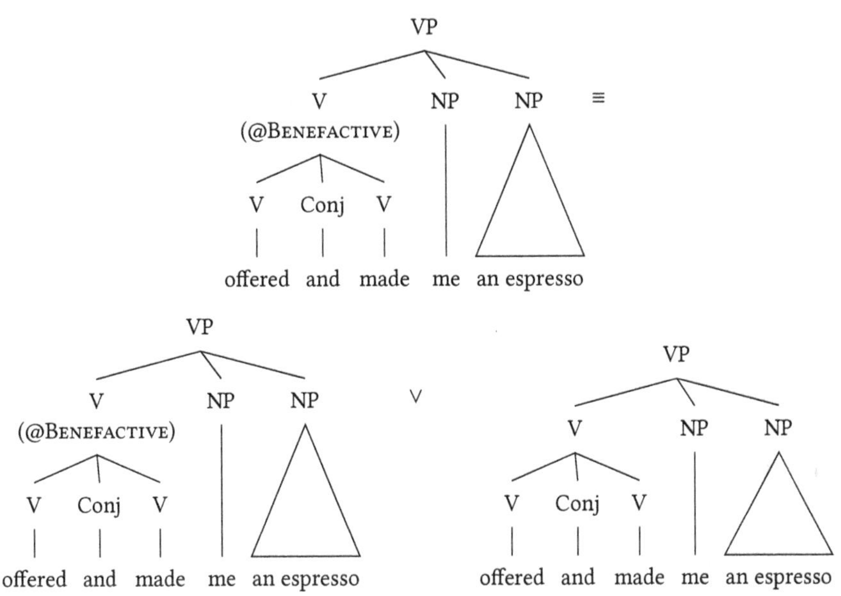

Figure 5.1: The optionality of a call of a template corresponds to a disjunction.

basically corresponds to the disjunction of the two trees in the lower part of the figure. The optionality does not allow for a distribution to one of the daughters in a coordination.

Mary Dalrymple (p. c. 2016) pointed out that the coordination rule that coordinates two verbs can be annotated with two optional calls of the benefactive template.

(59) V $\rightarrow$ V (@Benefactive) Conj V (@Benefactive)

In an analysis of the examples in (58), the template in rule (51) would not be called but the respective templates in (59) would be called instead. While this does work technically, similar coordination rules would be needed for all other constructions that introduce arguments in c-structures. Furthermore, the benefactive would have to be introduced in several unrelated places in the grammar and finally the benefactive is introduced at nodes consisting of a single verb without any additional arguments being licensed, which means that one could have gone for the lexical approach right away. Timm Lichte (p. c. 2016) pointed out an important consequence of a treatment of coordination via (59): since the result of the coordination behaves like a normal ditransitive verb it would enter the normal ditransitive construction and hence it would be predicted that none of the constraints on passive and extraction that are formulated at the phrasal level would hold if an item is coordinated with either another benefactive verb or a normal ditransitive verb like *give*. This is contrary to the facts: by coordinating items with strong restrictions with items with weaker restrictions, one gets a coordination structure that is at least as restrictive as the items that are coordinated. One does not get less restrictive by coordinating items.

The next section deals with German and explains in detail why cross-linguistic generalizations are not captured in the phrasal approach, but I want to mention two phenomena here since they are relevant to the point of missing language internal generalizations. As was shown in Müller (2006: Section 5), there is interaction between the resultative construction and nominalizations, which cannot be captured by inheritance. Similarly there are prenominal adjectival phrases in German that include resultatives and/or benefactives (Section 4, Section 6.1.3). For these phenomena, the interaction of the respective constructions follows immediately from a lexical approach while the interaction has to be stated on a case by case basis on the template-based phrasal approach. So, while the passive example above may be dealt with by underspecification, e.g., optionality of arguments, this is not possible for the nominalization structures since the syntax of NPs is really different from the syntax of verb phrases.

(60) a. [dass] jemand die Nordsee leer fischt
that somebody.NOM the.ACC North.Sea empty fishes

b. wegen der *Leerfischung* der Nordsee[3]
because of.the empty.fishing of.the North.Sea
'because of the fishing that resulted in the North Sea being empty'

In a phrasal world, transformations or meta-rules would be needed to capture the relation between the verbal and the nominal structures. Note that GPSG-style metarules relate local trees, that is, trees of depth one. The structure for the noun phrase in (60b) is something like (61) and more elaborate than a local tree.

[3] Example from the German newspaper taz, 20.06.1996, p. 6.

(61) [Det [[[Adj V] -ung]] NP[*gen*]]

This means that transformations with their full power would be needed to relate this structure to verbal structures. Such powerful transformations were abandoned in all branches of linguistics a long time ago (Chomsky 1981).

In summing up this section, it can be said that either the c-structure configurations do not contribute any constraints that are relevant for the analysis of argument structure constructions apart from the Benefactive template itself or they do and then there is a missing generalization since active and passive c-structures are unrelated.

To relate the c-structure rules or complete trees, one would need meta-rules or transformations, respectively. No such devices are needed in lexical approaches, in which complex structures are licensed by valence information of lexical items and abstract rules or schemata. Rather than relating rules that license certain structures or relating certain structures directly, lexical items are related by lexical rules.

6 Crosslinguistic generalizations

In Müller & Wechsler (2014a) we argued that the approach to Swedish caused motion constructions by Asudeh, Dalrymple & Toivonen (2008; 2013) would not carry over to German since the German construction interacts with derivational morphology. Asudeh & Toivonen (2014) argued that Swedish is different from German and hence there would not be a problem. However, the situation is different with the benefactive construction and with resultative constructions. Although English and German do differ in many respects, both languages have similar benefactive and resultative constructions.

In the following subsections I discuss the properties of these constructions in detail and show that a lexical account works for both German and English while a phrasal account does not extend to less configurational languages like German.

6.1 The benefactive construction

German has a benefactive construction that is rather similar to the English construction.

(62) a. He baked her a cake.

b. Er buk ihr einen Kuchen.
he.NOM baked her.DAT a.ACC cake

German differs from English in having a dative case and this affects phenomena like passivization, but in general the constructions are similar enough to make it worthwhile to look for crosslinguistic generalizations. In what follows, I look at ways to account for constituent structure in German and show that all imaginable ways are incompatible with approaches that assume that arguments are introduced in certain configurations.

6.1.1 Binary branching structures

The analysis of the free constituent order in German was explained by assuming binary branching structures in which a VP node is combined with one of its

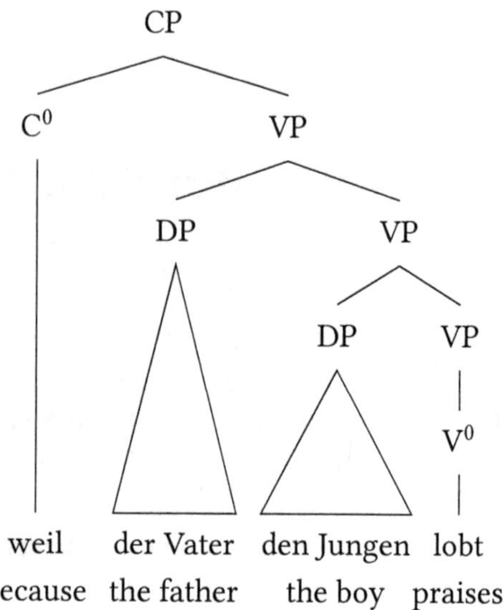

Figure 6.1: Analysis of German embedded clauses according to Berman (2003: 37)

arguments or adjuncts (see Berman 1996: Section 2.1.3.1; 2003 and also Choi 1999). For instance, Berman (2003: 37) assumes the analysis depicted in Figure 6.1. The c-structure rule for VP-argument combinations is provided in (63):

(63) VP $\rightarrow$ DP VP
$(\uparrow \text{SUBJ} \mid \text{OBJ} \mid \text{OBJ}_\theta) = \downarrow$ $\uparrow = \downarrow$

The dependent elements contribute to the f-structure of the verb and coherence/completeness ensure that all arguments of the verb are present. One could add the introduction of the benefactive argument to the VP node of the right-hand side of the rule as in (64):

(64) VP $\rightarrow$ DP VP
$(\uparrow \text{SUBJ} \mid \text{OBJ} \mid \text{OBJ}_\theta) = \downarrow$ $\uparrow = \downarrow$
(@BENEFACTIVE)

However, since the verb-final variant of (62b) would have the structure in (65), one would get spurious ambiguities: since the benefactive could be introduced at any of the three VP nodes in (65), one would get three analyses with exactly the same semantics.

(65) weil [$_{VP}$ er [$_{VP}$ ihr [$_{VP}$ einen Kuchen [$_{VP}$ [$_{V}$ buk]]]]]
because he.NOM her.DAT a.ACC cake baked

So the only way to avoid this seems to be to introduce the benefactive at the rule that got the recursion going, namely the rule in (66), which projects the lexical verb to the VP level.

(66) VP $\rightarrow$ (V)
$\uparrow = \downarrow$

But this unary branching rule is almost a lexical rule.

Note that there is a further problem for the template-based approach. The traceless approach to the verb position in German developed by Berman (2003) assumes that the verb is optional in (66). The optionality is marked by enclosing the V in brackets. Because of the optionality, there is nothing to attach the benefactive template to. Even if one would change the notational schema of LFG and allow for the attachment of f-structure constraints to mother nodes, this would not solve the problem since a principle that is called Economy of Expression (Bresnan 2001: 81; Bresnan, Asudeh, Toivonen & Wechsler 2015: 90) removes/avoids nodes without daughters.[1] The verb-initial variant of (65) is given in Figure 6.2. There is no verbal node to which one can attach the benefactive template and introducing it at the C node seems counter-intuitive. The natural place for it to be introduced is the verb since it has to be realized somewhere in the sentence. This is of course the lexical approach. Of course one could insist on introducing constraints regarding a benefactive argument at the projection in (66). For instance, one could assume that the V is optional and that the annotation is made at the VP. The result would be the structure at the right in Figure 6.2. The V is omitted, but the VP node has to be there since it contributes the benefactive constraints. So whether there are verb traces or not would depend on the presence of argument structure changing elements in the clause, a highly counter-intuitive outcome. Again, if the information about the benefactive argument is introduced lexically, the left structure in Figure 6.2 can be assumed and no additional assumptions are necessary.

As an alternative to introducing the benefactive template at a V or VP node, one could assume that the dative DP introduces the benefactive. Berman (2003) develops an analysis in which grammatical functions are assigned via implicational constraints that infer the grammatical function from the case of an NP/DP. Figure 6.3, which is a simplified version of the figure she discusses on p. 37, shows the implicational constraints and that they are attached to certain phrase structure positions. This proposal was criticized in Müller (2016a: Section 7.4) since

[1] "All syntactic phrase structure nodes are optional and are not used unless required by independent principles (completeness, coherence, semantic expressivity)." (Bresnan et al. 2015: 90)

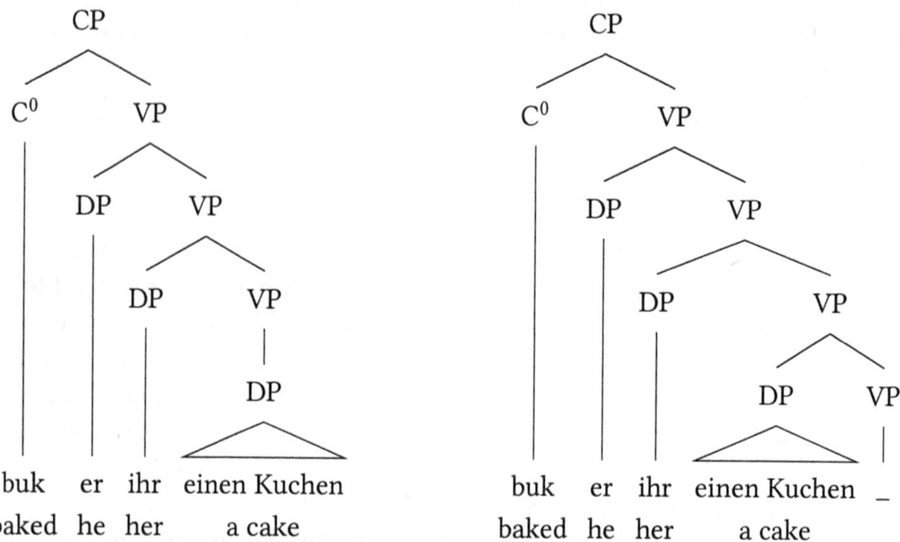

Figure 6.2: Left: Analysis of German verb-initial clauses in a co-head approach with empty nodes removed because of Economy of Expression according to Berman (2003: 41), Right: Analysis with VP introducing the benefactive template

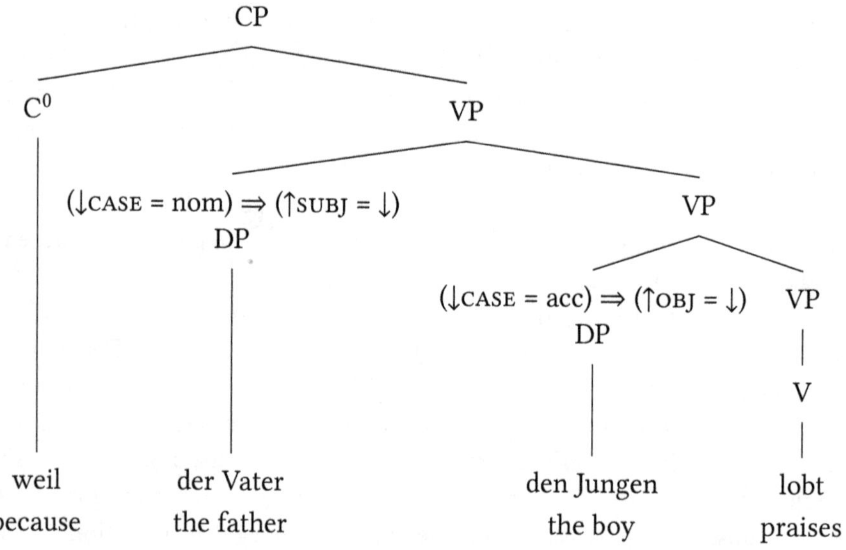

Figure 6.3: Correspondence between case and grammatical function according to Berman (2003: 37)

case in German cannot be unambiguously related to grammatical functions. In the case at hand the presence of a dative could be used to infer the grammatical function of a benefactive argument and hence find a natural place for the attachment of the benefactive template. However, the situation is not as simple as it first may appear. In examples like (67a) we have a so-called dative passive. The dative object is promoted to subject and hence gets nominative case. When verbal projections are embedded under AcI verbs, their subject is realized as accusative. (67b) shows an example of the embedding of the benefactive construction under an AcI verb in which the benefactive argument is realized as accusative. Finally, the nominalization in (67c) shows that the benefactive argument can be realized in the genitive as well.

(67) a. Der Mann bekam einen Kuchen gebacken.
the.NOM man got a.ACC cake baked

b. ? Peter ließ den Mann einen Kuchen gebacken bekommen und
Peter let the.ACC man a.ACC cake baked get and
kümmerte sich nicht darum.
cared REFL not there.around
'Peter permitted that the man got a cake baked and did not care about this.'

c. Das Kuchen-gebacken-Bekommen der Männer nervt mich.
the cake-backed-get the.GEN men nerve me
'The getting cake baked of the men annoys me.'

This can be accounted for straightforwardly in a lexical approach in which the dative is a dependent of *backen*. Either a lexical rule or the auxiliary verb takes care of the fact that the dative argument has to be realized as nominative in dative-passive constructions like (67a) (see Müller (2002: Section 3.2.3) for details of an auxiliary-based approach in HPSG). When dative-passives are embedded under AcI verbs, the subject becomes the object of the AcI verb and hence receives accusative. And finally, arguments with structural case that are realized in nominal environments get genitive, as in (67c). Nothing special has to be stipulated in the lexical approach. A phrasal approach that wants to assign semantic roles based on dative case is lost though.

Note also that the dative can be fronted across clause boundaries:

(68) Dieser Frau hat er behauptet, nie einen Kuchen zu backen.
this.DAT woman has he.NOM claimed never a.ACC cake to bake
'He claimed that he never bakes this woman a cake.'

A simple model that adds an OBJ_θ to the f-structure in which a dative appears would fail here, since the OBJ belongs into the f-structure of *backen* rather than into the f-structure of *behauptet.* This is due to the fact that the benefactive is extracted and not realized within the VP with the appropriate f-structure (*nie einen Kuchen zu backen* 'never a cake to bake'). The situation is depicted in Figure 6.4. So one would either have to assume a dative trace in the *backen* VP,

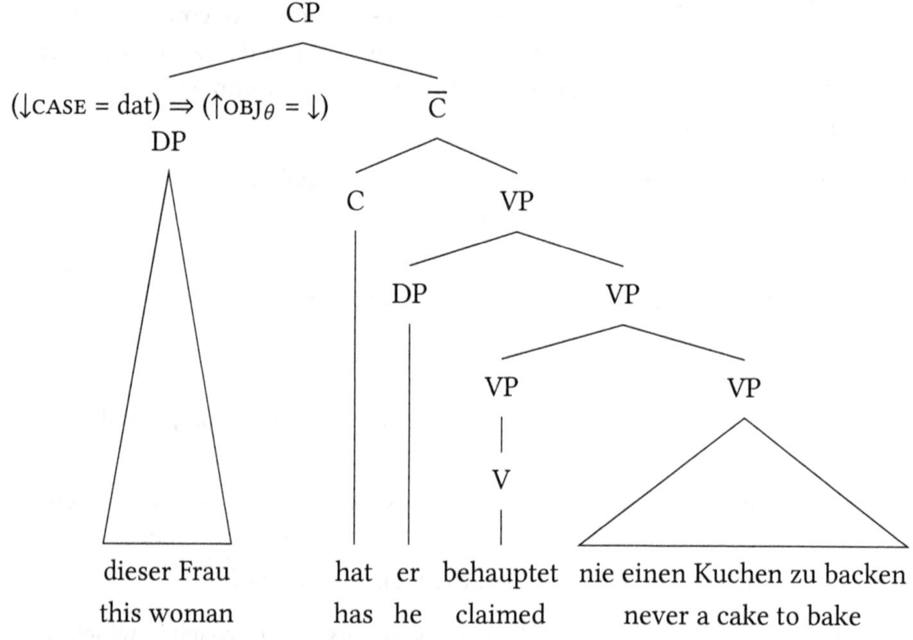

Figure 6.4: Benefactive construction with fronted dative. Assignment of grammatical functions based on case would exclude such structures

something that is usually not done, or functional uncertainty (Kaplan & Zaenen 1989) would be needed to find the right f-structure or σ structure. This means that benefactive arguments have to "know" where they could come from. This is an unwanted consequence since the treatment of nonlocal dependencies should be independent of the benefactive construction.

The examples in (67) show that the benefactive argument, which is realized as OBJ_θ in active sentences can be realized as SUBJ (68a) or as OBJ (68b). This means that one cannot assume a c-structure rule that combines an OBJ_θ DP with a verb and (optionally) attach the benefactive template to this DP. Rather one has to say that subjects, objects and secondary objects may be benefactive arguments. This means that one could assume that the benefactive template is optionally associated with the DP in the c-structure rule in (64), but this would result in the same spurious ambiguities that result from an attachment to the VP node.

6.1.2 Flat structures

A reviewer of Joint 2016 Conference on Head-driven Phrase Structure Grammar and Lexical Functional Grammar (HeadLex2016) suggested that flat structures could be assumed for German as well. The first problem with this is that most authors working in HPSG and LFG follow Haider (1993) in assuming that there is no IP/VP separation in German. For finite verbs it is assumed that subjects are realized in the verbal domain just like other arguments are (Berman 2003: Section 3.2.2, Section 3.2.3; Zaenen & Kaplan 2002: 412). So for German one would have to assume a c-structure rule that includes the subject (as Zaenen & Kaplan 2002: 412 do) and hence would have a rule that differs from the c-structure rule for English. A missed generalization.

6.1.2.1 Adjuncts

Furthermore, German differs from English in allowing adjuncts to appear everywhere between the arguments of a verb. So, all of the following sentences are possible:

(69) a. dass der Mann seiner Frau den Kuchen morgen bäckt
that the man his wife the cake tomorrow bakes
'that the man will bake his wife the cake tomorrow'

b. dass der Mann seiner Frau morgen den Kuchen bäckt
that the man his wife tomorrow the cake bakes
'that the man will bake his wife the cake tomorrow'

c. dass der Mann morgen seiner Frau den Kuchen bäckt
that the man tomorrow his wife the cake bakes
'that the man will bake his wife the cake tomorrow'

d. dass morgen der Mann seiner Frau den Kuchen bäckt
that tomorrow the man his wife the cake bakes
'that the man will bake his wife the cake tomorrow'

As Uszkoreit (1987) has shown, all adjunct positions can be filled simultaneously and it is also possible to have more than one adjunct per adjunct position. The modified flat c-structure would look as in (70):[2]

[2]See Uszkoreit (1987: 146) and Kasper (1994) for similar flat rules in GPSG and HPSG, respectively.

(70) $$\mathrm{V}' \rightarrow \begin{array}{cccc} \mathrm{XP}^{*} & (\mathrm{DP}) & \mathrm{XP}^{*} & (\mathrm{DP}) \\ \downarrow \in (\uparrow \textsc{adj}) & (\uparrow \textsc{subj}) = \downarrow & \downarrow \in (\uparrow \textsc{adj}) & (\uparrow \textsc{obj}) = \downarrow \\ \\ \mathrm{XP}^{*} & (\mathrm{DP}) & \mathrm{XP}^{*} & (\mathrm{V}) \\ \downarrow \in (\uparrow \textsc{adj}) & (\uparrow \textsc{obj}_{\theta}) = \downarrow & \downarrow \in (\uparrow \textsc{adj}) & \uparrow = \downarrow \\ & & & (\ @\textsc{Benefactive}\ ) \end{array}$$

The '*' stands for arbitrarily many repetitions. While this rule works for German, it is inappropriate for English. One could say that English has a more specific version of this rule, namely a rule in which the number of possible adjuncts is specified to be zero. However, this would beg the question how the more general rule could play a role in the grammar of English. One would have to stipulate that the language acquisition process somehow involves rules like (70) but the English speaking children have to find out that they cannot use adjuncts in the respective slots. This is implausible if one does not want to assume that rules like (70) are innate and language learners derive more specific instances from them. So, again there are differences in the grammars of German and English that prevent phrasal approaches from capturing the commonalities of argument structure constructions.

6.1.2.2 Scrambling

German differs from English in allowing for almost free orderings of arguments. This also affects benefactives as is shown by (71):

(71) a. dass der Mann seiner Frau einen Kuchen bäckt
that the man his wife a cake bakes
'that the man bakes his wife a cake'

b. dass der Mann einen Kuchen seiner Frau bäckt
that the man a cake his wife bakes
'that the man bakes his wife a cake'

c. dass dieser Frau jeder Mann einen Kuchen bäckt
that this woman every man a cake bakes
'that every man bakes this woman a cake'

d. dass dieser Frau solchen Kuchen niemand bäckt
that this woman such.a cake nobody bakes
'that nobody bakes this woman such a cake'

e. dass einen Kuchen dieser Frau niemand bäckt
that a cake this woman nobody bakes
'that nobody bakes this woman a cake'

f. dass einen Kuchen niemand dieser Frau bäckt
that a cake nobody this woman bakes
'that nobody bakes this woman a cake'

This can be captured by either stating six c-structure rules that all involve the benefactive template or by using just one c-structure rule that does not specify the grammatical functions of the involved DPs. See Zaenen & Kaplan (2002: 413) for the latter approach.[3] In any case the c-structure rule or rules would differ from what was assumed for English and there would be no way to capture the generalization.

6.1.2.3 Verbal complexes

Apart from these differences between English and German, phrasal accounts are challenged by the fact that the verb may be separated from the benefactive DP/NP by an auxiliary:

(72) dass er ihr einen Kuchen wird backen müssen
that he.NOM her.DAT a.ACC cake will bake must
'that it will be necessary for him to bake her a cake'

Sentences like (72) are usually analyzed by assuming that *backen* and *müssen* form a verbal complex, which is in turn embedded under the future auxiliary *wird* (Bech 1955; Hinrichs & Nakazawa 1989; 1994; Haider 1990; Kiss 1995; Meurers 1999a; Kathol 2001; Müller 1999; 2002; Berman 2003: Section 3.2.4; Forst & Rohrer 2009). The complete verbal complex is combined with *einen Kuchen*, *ihr* and *er*. There have been proposals for a flat analysis of sentences containing a verbal complex (Bouma & van Noord 1998) but these relied on argument attraction and suggested a very general dominance schema. Of course one could (optionally) add the benefactive template to a very general schema but this solution would not be an implementation of the pattern-based constructional approaches in which it is assumed that certain specific configurations license the introduction of specific arguments.

[3] A simplified version of Zaenen & Kaplan's rule is given in Footnote 6. Their rule only deals with NPs/DPs. German also allows for the scrambling of PPs, APs, VPs and even CPs. So the category and the grammatical functions that are assigned in such a general rule for the German clause have to be more inclusive.

Note that the benefactive template cannot be attached to the VP node or to the dative DP. The benefactive template would add arguments to the σ-structure of *wird* since *backen* is embedded under *wird* and *müssen*. *wird* introduces a tense relation and *müssen* a modal operator. Depending on the analysis of the semantic structure, the ARG2 and ARG3 referred to in the BENEFACTIVE template would end up in the σ structure of *wird* or *müssen* rather than in the σ structure of *backen*.[4]

To make things even more complicated for the phrasal account, the verbal complexes can be coordinated. (73) illustrates:

(73) dass er ihr einen Kuchen wird backen müssen oder hat backen sollen
that he.NOM her.DAT a.ACC cake will bake must or has bake shall
'that it will be necessary for him to bake her a cake or that he should bake her a cake'

Such sentences can be accounted for easily if one assumes that *wird backen müssen* and *hat backen sollen* form verbal complexes which are then coordinated and finally combined with the other NPs/DPs in the sentence. The structure for (72) with a flat VP including the subject is given in Figure 6.5 on the facing page.[5]

Bresnan et al. (1982) developed an account of cross-serial dependencies that explains sentences like (74) by assuming that objects and prepositional objects are part of a verbless VP with the verb being realized in the verbal complex.

(74) dat Jan Piet Marie de kinderen zag helpen laten zwemmen
that Jan Piet Marie the children saw help let swim
'that Jan saw Piet help Marie make the children swim'

Since both the content of the verbless VP and the respective verb in the verbal complex are mapped to the same f-structure (the VCOMP value of the respective mother node), the objects are mapped to the correct f-structure. Since there is a VP in this account one could be tempted to believe that this account could be extended to German and a resultative or benefactive VP could be assumed for German, which would make the argument above irrelevant.

[4] This is not a problem for grammatical functions in f-structures since raising predicates are assumed to have additional slots for raised arguments, but this should not be the case for semantic representations.

[5] This structure is equivalent, modulo node names, to what Zaenen & Kaplan's rules (2002: 413) would license. Zaenen & Kaplan's rule incorporate a linearization constraint that prevents orders in the verbal complex in which the governing verb is not final. So they exclude so-called Auxiliary Flip. But this can be fixed easily.

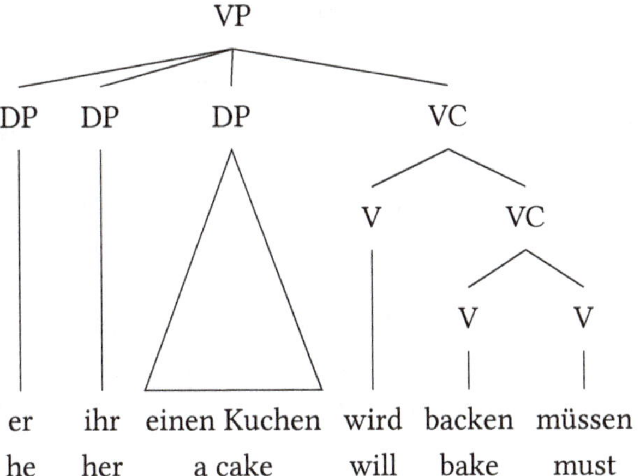

Figure 6.5: Analysis of German clause involving a verbal complex and a flat clausal structure

I do not want to discuss the details of Bresnan et al.'s proposal here but simply want to point out that it would not extend to German since, first, subjects can be scrambled with other arguments so a VP without the subject would not be an appropriate unit to begin with and, second, subjects of higher verbs may be scrambled with objects of embedded verbs, as is demonstrated by the examples in (75):

(75) a. dass den Mann seiner Frau solchen Kuchen niemand backen sah
that the.ACC man his.DAT wife such.ACC cake nobody.NOM bake saw
'that nobody saw the man bake his wife such a cake'

b. dass den Mann niemand seiner Frau solchen Kuchen backen sah
that the.ACC man nobody.NOM his.DAT wife such cake bake saw
'that nobody saw the man bake his wife such a cake'

c. dass solchen Kuchen niemand den Mann seiner Frau backen sah
that such.ACC cake nobody.NOM the.ACC man his.DAT wife bake saw

These are three examples exemplifying the phenomenon but in principle all permutations of arguments belonging to verbs of a verbal complex are possible. Of course there are problems with arguments of the same case when there is not sufficient context information to resolve which argument fills which role, but this is also the case with simplex verbs. See Müller (1999: Section 11.4) for discussion.

The point about these examples is that unless one is willing to include the subject of AcI verbs among the daughters of a very flat phrase structure rule, there is no way to model sentences like (75) with a flat rule for benefactives like (56) or (70) and continuous constituents.[6]

Having a rule that combines *backen* with four NPs is highly implausible though, since the nominative depends on the AcI verb and not on *backen*. In any case such a rule would be inappropriate for English. See also Müller (2006: Section 2.5) for examples of the interaction of AcI verbs with resultative constructions.

6.1.2.4 Coordination, fronting and partial structures

Forst & Rohrer (2009) assume a flat VP for German to account for certain coordination structures. However, their theory of coordination assumes partial VPs. In the analysis of (76), the VP *seiner Frau buk* 'his wife baked' would be coordinated with *seiner Tochter zeigte* 'his daughter showed'.

---

[6]The rule in (i) is an adapted version of the rule that Zaenen & Kaplan (2002: 413) use to describe sentences with verbal complexes:

(i) $\text{VP} \rightarrow \underset{(\uparrow \text{COMP}^* \text{ NGF}) = \downarrow}{\text{DP}^*} \quad \underset{\uparrow = \downarrow}{(\text{V}')}$

The '*' after the DP symbol means that there can be arbitrarily many DPs. The grammatical function that is filled by the DPs is not specified. It is just specified that the DP has to fill an NGF, where NGF stands for *nominal grammatical function*, that is SUBJ, OBJ, OBJ2, …. The COMP* ensures that the specification of the nominal grammatical function can reach any feature structure at the end of a path of several COMPS. This solves the problem that *einen Kuchen* in (72) is the object of *backen*. By using the functional uncertainty it is possible to assign the OBJ function to the f-structure of *backen*. But note that this schema is very general. Mentioning benefactives on either the DP or the V′ would not capture the constraints that are supposed to be associated with a constructional pattern for benefactives. Independent of where the benefactive template is introduced one would need functional uncertainties to find an appropriate verb in the verbal complex.

Note furthermore that Zaenen & Kaplan's rule is too simple. Their rule and the version provided here only admits NPs/DPs before the verbal complex but German allows for NPs, PPs, APs and even VPs and CPs and there is no fixed order of these elements. So rather than specifying DP* and appropriate grammatical function assignments, one would have to specify (DP|PP|AP|VP|CP)* and appropriate grammatical functions.

In any case the idea of isolating a constructional pattern for benefactives would not be captured by such a proposal and again the rule in (i) and possible adaptions are very different from the c-structure rule for English.

(76) dass er den Kuchen [seiner Frau buk] und [seiner Tochter
that he.NOM the.ACC cake his.DAT wife baked but his.DAT daughter
zeigte]
showed
'that he baked his wife a cake and showed it to his daughter'

These partial VPs are parallel to the VPs in approaches with binary branching. Any LFG analysis of German has to admit such partial VPs since German allows for partial VP fronting:[7]

(77) a. [Seiner Frau backen] würde er solche Kuchen niemals.
his.DAT wife bake would he.NOM such.ACC cakes never
'He would never bake such cakes for his wife.'

b. [Solche Kuchen backen] würde er seiner Frau niemals.
such.ACC cakes bake would he.NOM his.DAT wife never

c. [Backen] würde er seiner Frau solche Kuchen niemals,
bake would he.NOM his.DAT wife such.ACC cakes never
kaufen schon.
buy PART
'He would never bake his wife such a cake, but he would buy one.'

Hence the idea that the benefactive is introduced in a special phrase structural configuration together with a verb and all other objects would not work for German. See Nerbonne (1986) and Johnson (1986), who introduced lexical valence representations in a Categorial Grammar style into GPSG since there was no way to make the phrasal GPSG approach compatible with German partial VP fronting data.

Note also that such frontings can occur with a modal as main verb:

(78) [Einen solchen Kuchen backen] musste er seiner Frau noch nie.
a.ACC such cake bake must he.NOM his.DAT wife yet never
'He never had to bake his wife such a cake.'

Such examples also pose problems for adding f-structure information since the dative appears in the domain of the modal rather than the domain of the main verb (see previous paragraph).

None of these data poses a problem for standard LFG: the lexical analysis of benefactives that was suggested by Toivonen (2013) interacts with the analysis

[7] Again see Zaenen & Kaplan (2002) for an account of partial VP fronting in German in the framework of LFG.

of partial verb phrase frontings suggested by Zaenen & Kaplan (2002) without further ado.

6.1.3 Other environments

Note also that benefactive datives appear in adjectival environments as in (79):

(79) a. der seiner Frau einen Kuchen backende Mann
the his.DAT wife a.ACC cake baking man
'the man who is baking a cake for his wife'

b. der einen Kuchen seiner Frau backende Mann
the a.ACC cake his.DAT wife baking man
'the man who is baking a cake for his wife'

The examples in (79) show that the arguments of *backende* may be scrambled, as is common in verbal environments.

In order to account for these datives one would have to assume that the adjective-to-AP rule that would be parallel to (66) introduces the dative. The semantics of the benefactive template ensures that the benefactive argument is not added to intransitive verbs like *lachen* 'to laugh' or participles like *lachende* 'laughing'. While this is a possible analysis, I find the overall approach unattractive. First, it does not have anything to do with the original constructional proposal but just states that the benefactive may be introduced at several places in syntax. Second, the unary branching syntactic rule applies to a lexical item and hence is very similar to a lexical rule. Third, the analysis does not capture cross-linguistic commonalities of the construction. In a lexical rule-based approach such as the one that was suggested by Briscoe & Copestake (1999: Section 5), Cook (2006), Kibort (2008), and Toivonen (2013), a benefactive argument is added to certain verbs and the lexical rule is parallel in all languages that have this phenomenon. The respective languages just differ in the way the arguments are realized in respect to their heads. In languages that have adjectival participles, these are derived from the respective verbal stems. The morphological rule is general and does not refer to benefactive arguments and the syntactic rules for adjectival phrases do not have to mention benefactive arguments either.

6.1.4 Summary

I showed in this section that it is not viable to introduce the benefactive argument in binary branching structures since there is no canonical place for doing so. Introducing it at the VP recursion results in spurious ambiguities. Introducing it at the rule that gets the recursion going is almost equivalent to the lexical approach and in any case it would not have anything to do with a specific configuration that licenses the construction. Making the benefactive template dependent on the presence of a DP/NP with a certain case fails for several reasons: first, the benefactive argument may be realized in various cases and, second, it may be realized far away from its canonical place and hence all constraints referring to the f-structure or the σ structure would potentially address wrong structures because of nonlocal dependencies. I furthermore showed that flat structures are not an option either since partial structures are needed for partial verb phrase fronting and coordination, and in any case flat structures may be interrupted by verbal complexes that embed the main verb under modal operators, again leading to the inaccessibility of the relevant f-structures and σ structures.

The lexical approach adds information right at the place where the necessary information is accessible. None of the discussed problems affects the lexical approach.

6.2 Resultative constructions

Having discussed the benefactive construction, I now turn to Christie's analysis of resultative constructions. Christie (2010) suggests the following c-structure rule for resultatives in English:

(80)
$$\begin{array}{llccc} V' & \rightarrow & V & DP & \{\,DP|AP|PP\,\} \\ & & \uparrow = \downarrow & (\uparrow \textsc{obj}) = \downarrow & (\uparrow \textsc{xcomp}) = \downarrow \\ & & & & (\downarrow\textsc{subj}) = (\uparrow\textsc{obj}) \\ & & & & @\textsc{result-t}((\uparrow\textsc{pred fn})) \end{array}$$

Christie claims that the result predicate cannot be extracted. According to her examples like (81) are ungrammatical (p. 157):

(81) ? Pink, Kim dyed her hair.

She rates the example with a '?' rather than a '*', but examples of this kind have been frequently cited in the literature as well-formed (see also the discussion of (37) on p. 23) and corpus examples like (82a) can be found:

(82) a. What Color Should You Dye Your Hair?[8]
b. How flat did John hammer the metal?[9]

[8] http://www.gurl.com/2011/06/28/quiz-what-color-should-you-dye-your-hair-beauty/, 2016-05-28.

[9] Roberts (1988: 115).

Examples like (81) and (82) are usually treated by functional uncertainty. The element that is extracted is declared to be optional in the c-structure. The f-structure slot is filled via a functional uncertainty equation. The problem with an optional result phrase in (81) is that (81) could be used to analyze simple verb phrases of strictly transitive verbs. This would result in two analyses of sentences with transitive verbs with exactly the same f-structure. A clearly unwanted result. Of course one could argue that the rule in (80) is supposed to cover both strictly transitive verbs and transitive verbs with a result predicate, but this would not capture the original constructional idea that the phrasal configuration somehow is connected to the meaning contributed by the pattern (Goldberg 1995; Goldberg & Jackendoff 2004). The problem with result predicate extraction could be fixed by shifting the call to the RESULT-T template to the verb since the verb cannot be extracted. However, this shifting the template to the verb would not help in the case of German. German V2 and V1 clauses are usually analyzed as involving head-movement of the verb. C and V are treated as co-heads and the functional information is contributed by the finite verb in C rather than by an empty element in the VP. The analysis is shown in Figure 6.6. The consequence of this is

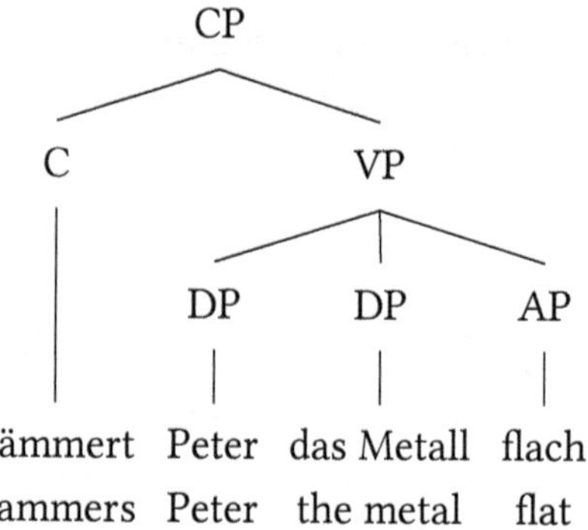

Figure 6.6: Analysis of a V1 sentence with verb-position via C/V co-heads and an English-style flat VP

that all elements that would be part of a resultative VP can in fact be realized outside of this VP: the subject, the object and the result can be extracted and the verb can be realized in C. To illustrate this, the elements that are missing from the VP are indicated by $\_{i}$ and $\_{j}$ in (83):

(83) a. Peter$_i$ hämmert$_j$ [$_{\text{VP}}$ $\_{i}$ das Metal flach $\_{j}$].
Peter hammers the metal flat

b. Das Metal$_i$ hämmert$_j$ [$_{VP}$ Peter _$_i$ flach _$_j$].
   the metal hammers Peter flat

c. Flach$_i$ hämmert$_j$ Peter [$_{VP}$ das Metal _$_i$ _$_j$].
   flat hammers Peter the metal

Hence, there is no reliable element to attach the resultative template to. The only sensible option seems to be the extension of LFG's c-structure annotation conventions: the resultative template would be added to the mother node of the VP.

Furthermore, German differs from English in forming verbal complexes, as was already discussed in Section 6.1.2.3. Müller (2002: Section 5.1) argued that result adjectives should also be treated as part of the predicate complex. Hence, the structure of (84a) differs from the one of the corresponding English example.

(84) a. dass er das Metal flach hämmert
     b. that he hammers the metal flat

The respective structures are shown in Figure 6.7. As explained above, both the

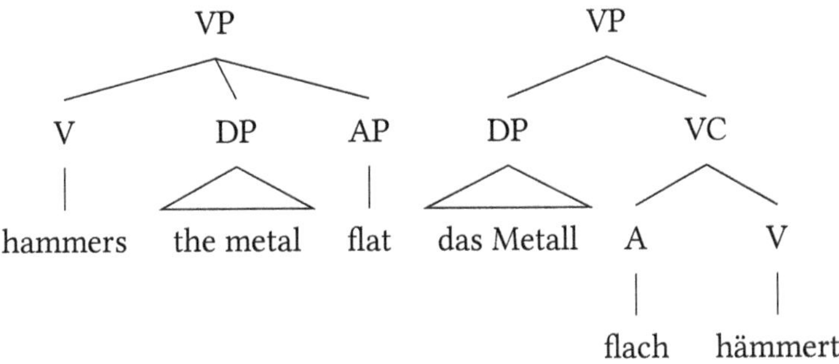

Figure 6.7: Resultative structures in English and German with a verbal complex for German

adjective and the verb and even adjective and verb simultaneously may be realized outside of the verbal complex, so there is no reliable element to attach the resultative template too. One could attach it to the mother node of the verbal complex but this would not include the object as in English or one could attach it to the VP dominating the object and the verbal complex but the latter proposal could not even enforce the presence of a result predicate of a certain category and a verb since adjective, verb and object are not in the same local tree.

In the lexical approach the template is combined with the verb directly both in German and in English (and other languages). The verb can be realized in C or in V. It contributes valence information to the f-structure that belongs to the V projection either as head or co-head and this ensures that the result predicate and the object has to be present in the f-structure. Extracted elements are contributed to the f-structure via functional uncertainty.

Concluding this subsection, it can be said that the fact that result adjectives form a verbal complex in German while they are part of the VP in English could not be covered if the use of templates required similar structures cross-linguistically. The lexical approach, on the other hand, does not have problems since the lexicon just states which arguments are needed leaving the actual realization to the syntax, which may be different from language to language.

6.3 Interaction between the benefactive and the resultative construction

As was already pointed out in Müller (2006: 861), the benefactive construction and the resultative construction interact. The example in (85c) shows that both a dative argument and an accusative argument may be added to the valence representation of a verb.

(85) a. [dass] er fischt
that he fishes

b. * [dass] er ihm fischt
that he him fishes

c. [dass] er ihm den Teich leer fischt
that he.NOM him.DAT the.ACC pond empty fishes

In order to cover this in a phrasal analysis, one would need a resultative/benefacti c-structure rule like (86):[10]

(86) V′ →

(DP)	(DP)	(DP)
(↑ SUBJ) = ↓	(↑ OBJ) = ↓	(↑ OBJ$_\theta$) = ↓

({AP|PP})	(V)
(↑ XCOMP) = ↓	↑ = ↓
(@RESULT-T((↑PRED FN)))	(@BENEFACTIVE)

The interesting thing about this rule is that all items on the right-hand side are optional. The rule licenses any combination of these items. In order to avoid

[10] This ignores the possibility of inserting adjuncts and the option to scramble the DP arguments.

overgeneration, it has to be made sure that exactly the right combination of items is present. This is ensured by the templates that regulate which grammatical functions have to be realized. The c-structure does not play any role in this business. Hence we could also assume a lexical approach and even return to binary branching structures: with binary branching structures each subtree licenses a head with an adjunct or an argument and it is either the f-structure + coherence and completeness or the glue semantics that has to make sure that all needed and only those arguments are present.

Note also that the combination of the benefactive and the resultative is hardly acceptable in English (Bresnan & Zaenen 1990: 53; Bresnan, Asudeh, Toivonen & Wechsler 2015: 339) and Norwegian (Tungseth 2007).

(87) * He fished him the pond empty.

So this means that the constituents in the right-hand side of the rule in (86) may never be realized simultaneously, if we want to assume this rule for both German and English. This is a very strange situation for a phrase structure rule indeed, even more so for a constructional theory. Note also that the rule in (86) could not be learned by speakers of English since they never hear all components simultaneously. The generalization that has to be captured is that benefactives may be added to verbs with an accusative object and that accusative objects and result predicates may be added to intransitive verbs. Lexical rule-based approaches cover this. The two phenomena are independently covered by two lexical rules: the benefactive lexical rule requires a verb that governs the accusative and adds an argument as second argument, which is realized as dative in German. The resultative lexical rule that is needed for the examples discussed above takes an intransitive verb as input and licenses one that governs an accusative and a result predicate. This is the same across several languages. What is different is the interaction between the rules. While German does allow benefactives with resultative constructions, English does not permit this. So the English rule is more constrained, but the general form of the rules is similar and generalizations can be captured.

6.4 Summary

I showed in this section that it is difficult to find places for the attachment of the benefactive and resultative templates in phrasal LFG analyses. Even if it was straightforward to find attachment sites, the respective c-structures would be different in English and German. While having different c-structures for different languages is common in LFG and not a problem per se, associating the benefactive and resultative construction with totally different configurations in the descriptions of the two languages misses a generalization. What has to be accounted for is that we have the same type of dependency in both languages and this can be expressed in valence representations in lexical items that interact with syntactic rules of the respective languages (Müller 2017a).

7 A lexical approach that can capture the cross-linguistic generalizations

This book has argued for a return to lexical analyses. Analyses of the respective phenomena have been worked out in LFG by Simpson (1983), Bresnan & Zaenen (1990) and Christie (2015) for resultative constructions in English and Cook (2006), Kibort (2008) and Toivonen (2013) for English benefactives. These analyses assume lexical items with a certain a-structure and related items with a different a-structure. I could point to these well-established analyses and leave it at that, but I want to use the remainder of the book to work out a detailed analysis of the phenomena that have been mentioned throughout the book and explain how their interactions are captured. The underlying framework that is assumed is Constructional HPSG (Sag 1997) with the basic assumptions regarding German and more generally Germanic made in Müller (2013a; 2015a; 2018a). The analysis is able to capture generalizations about the benefactive construction across the Germanic languages, something that is not possible in LFG since the labels for the arguments (ARG_2 and ARG_3) and the grammatical functions of the benefactive argument are different in German and English.

(88) a. He baked her a cake.

b. Er buk ihr einen Kuchen.
he.NOM baked her.DAT a.ACC cake

While *her* is ARG_2 and OBJ, the corresponding object in German is ARG_3 and OBJ_θ in German. This distinction is important since *her* can be promoted to subject (for speakers who allow for the passive), but *ihr*, being dative, cannot be promoted to subject in the normal agentive passive. In what follows, I show how the commonalities between (88a) and (88b) can be accounted for.

What is needed is basically two lexical rules: one for the introduction of the benefactive argument and one for the introduction of resultative predicates and the respective object. In addition, we of course need syntactic schemata that license the structures of German and English. These schemata are maximally simple. Four schemata are relevant in the context of this book: 1) the Specifier-Head Schema, 2) the Head-Complement Schema, 3) the Filler-Head Schema and 4) the Predicate Complex Schema.

7.1 Phrase structure, argument structure mappings and scrambling

7.1.1 Argument structure mappings

I assume that all lexical items come with a list that contains their arguments, the so-called argument structure list (ARG-ST). The elements of this list are mapped to valence features. In English and other SVO languages the first element of the ARG-ST list is mapped to the SPECIFIER feature (SPR) and all other arguments are mapped to the COMPLEMENTS list (COMPS). In German and other SOV languages all arguments of finite verbs are mapped to COMPS and the value of the SPR feature is the empty list. The lexical items in (89) illustrate:

(89) a. lexical entry for the stem *give*:

$$\begin{bmatrix} \text{SPR} & \boxed{1} \left\langle \text{NP}[\textit{nom}]_i \right\rangle \\ \text{COMPS} & \boxed{2} \left\langle \text{NP}[\textit{acc}]_j, \text{NP}[\textit{acc}]_k \right\rangle \\ \text{ARG-ST} & \boxed{1} \oplus \boxed{2} \end{bmatrix}$$

b. lexical entry for the stem of *geben* ‘give’:

$$\begin{bmatrix} \text{SPR} & \langle\, \rangle \\ \text{COMPS} & \boxed{1} \\ \text{ARG-ST} & \boxed{1} \left\langle \text{NP}[\textit{nom}]_i, \text{NP}[\textit{dat}]_j, \text{NP}[\textit{acc}]_k \right\rangle \end{bmatrix}$$

Both argument structure lists have the same order, corresponding to agent, recipient and theme. Because of this, the linking constraints for both English and German are parallel and generalizations are captured. The languages differ in how the arguments are realized: In English the first argument is mapped to the SPR list ($\boxed{1}$) and the others to COMPS ($\boxed{2}$), while in German, the complete ARG-ST list ($\boxed{1}$) is mapped to COMPS. Several authors have argued that there is no structural difference between subjects and objects of finite verbs in languages like German (Haider 1993: Section 6.3; Eisenberg 1994: 376; Berman (2003: 36–37)) and this claim is reflected by treating subjects as complements.

7.1.2 Phrase structure rules

The Figures 7.1 and 7.2 show how the lexical items can be used in actual analyses.

I assume binary branching structures for both German and English. English, being a VO language, is assumed to combine the head with the first element on the COMPS list first, while in the analysis of the German example the last element of the COMPS list is combined first with the head.

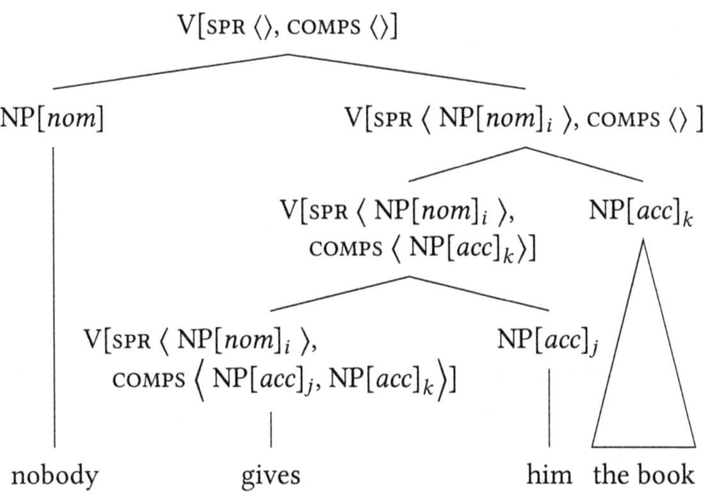

Figure 7.1: Analysis of an English example with a ditransitive verb

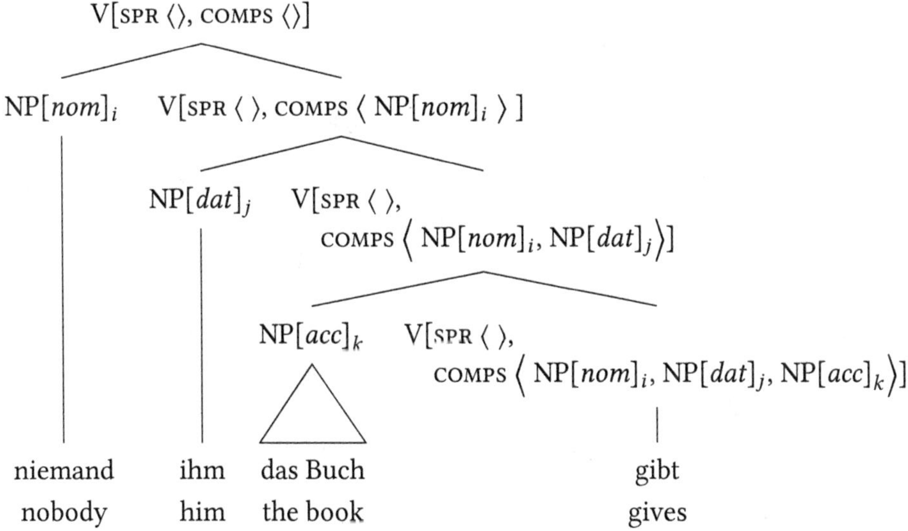

Figure 7.2: Analysis of a German example with a ditransitive verb

The schemata that license these structures are shown in Figure 7.3 and 7.4. Figure 7.3 shows a sketch of the Specifier-Head Schema, which licenses structures with a specifier. These are subject-VP combinations in English and determiner-$\overline{\text{N}}$ combinations in both English and German. The figure shows that the SPR list of

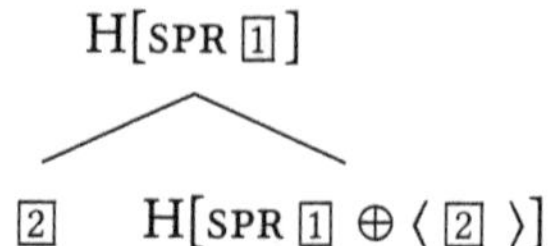

Figure 7.3: Sketch of the Specifier-Head Schema

the head (marked by H) is split into two parts: a list with exactly one element (2) and a rest (1) (⊕ stands for list concatenation). 2 has to match the element that is combined with the head. The remaining list (1) is the value of the SPR list of the mother node. Usually this list is the empty list, but see Müller & Ørsnes (2013) for an analysis of object shift in Danish where multiple specifiers are assumed.

Figure 7.4 shows the Head-Complement Schema as it would be needed for English. The COMPS list of the head is split into two lists. One contains exactly

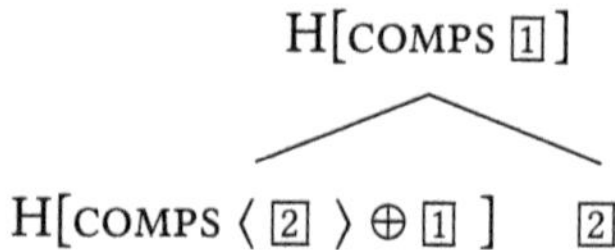

Figure 7.4: Sketch of the Head-Complement Schema

one element, the element that is combined with the head (2). The remainder of the list is passed up to the COMPS list of the mother.

For German, I assume that adjuncts may attach to any verbal projection (to be precise, to any verb-final projection) and in English adjuncts may attach to VPs. Because of the binary branching structures, the fact that adjuncts can appear anywhere between arguments in German is accounted for. Adjuncts do not have to be mentioned in argument structure constructions, as would be the case in phrasal models of German syntax assuming flat structures (see (70) on page 48).

7.1.3 Scrambling

Now, German differs from English in allowing scrambling. Rather than having a fixed constituent order as in English, German allows for six order variants of sentences with verbs with three arguments (see (71) on page 48). This can be allowed for by relaxing the order in which heads are combined with their arguments. The more general schema is provided in Figure 7.5.

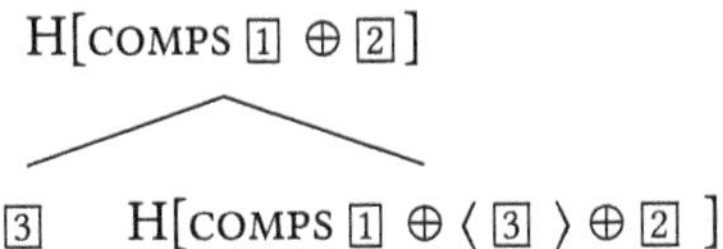

Figure 7.5: Sketch of the Head-Complement Schema for languages with free constituent order

In this version of the Head-Complement Schema the COMPS list of the head is split into three lists: the two lists $\boxed{1}$ and $\boxed{2}$ and a list in the middle that contains exactly one element ($\boxed{3}$). $\boxed{3}$ is combined with the head and the COMPS list of the mother contains all remaining complements, namely $\boxed{1}$ ⊕ $\boxed{2}$. This general schema allows for various instantiations: $\boxed{1}$ and $\boxed{2}$ may contain elements or be empty. If $\boxed{1}$ is empty, we get VO languages with strict order and if $\boxed{2}$ is empty, we get OV languages with strict order. This gives the nice result that the grammar of English is more restrictive than the one of German, since the schema for English is basically the same as in Figure 7.5 but with the additional constraint that $\boxed{1}$ is the empty list.

7.2 Lexical items and lexical rules

In what follows, I briefly discuss case assignment and linking. For a more detailed discussion of case assignment see Müller (2007a: Chapter 14).

7.2.1 Structural and lexical case

The following lexical items and lexical rules assume a distinction between structural and lexical case. Roughly speaking, structural case is case that is assigned in certain structures, that is, case that may change. In contrast, lexical case does not depend on the environment a lexical item is used in. I assume that verbal arguments that are realized as nominative and accusative in active sentences bear structural case. Following Haider (1986), the dative in German is treated as a lexical case. (90) shows examples of structural cases:

(90) a. Der Teich ist leer.
the pond is empty

b. Er fischt den Teich leer.
he fishes the pond empty

c. Der Teich wird leer gefischt.
the pond is empty fished
'the pond is fished empty'

d. das Leerfischen des Teiches
the empty.fishing the pond
'the fishing of the pond empty'

Case is assigned according to the following case principle (Przepiórkowski 1999; Meurers 1999b):[1]

Principle 1 (Case Principle)

- In a list that contains both subjects and complements of a verbal head, the first element with structural case is assigned nominative case unless it is raised to a dominating head.
- All other elements of this list with structural case are assigned accusative case.
- In nominal environments all elements with structural case are assigned genitive case.

This principle is not specific to German and English. It accounts for the case assignment of many languages, for instance Icelandic (Müller 2018a) and also Hindi (Müller 2015b).

7.2.2 Linking

(89) showed the argument structure of *give* and how the elements of the ARG-ST list are distributed to the valence features. Assuming the distinction between lexical and structural cases, we have the ARG-ST value in (91). The referential indices of the NP arguments are linked to semantic roles of the predicate *geben*. Instead of traditional role names like agent, recipient and theme, I use the features ARG1, ARG2 and ARG3.[2] ARG0 is the event variable, also represented as the

[1]This Case Principle is a declarative version of the case assignment theory that was developed by Yip, Maling & Jackendoff (1987).

[2]Since semantic relations correspond to types and types are specified for the features that are appropriate for objects of the type, it follows that ARG1, ARG2 and ARG3 are always present in feature structures of type *geben*. The AVM in (91) corresponds to the more canonical notation $geben(x, y, z)$, where x is ARG1, y is ARG2 and z is ARG3.

There are alternative ways to label the arguments. Authors like Davis & Koenig (2000) use the terms ACTOR and UNDERGOER. For worked out linking theories in HPSG see Wechsler (1991), Davis & Koenig (2000) and Sheinfux et al. (2016).

INDEX (IND) under CONTENT (CONT). Due to space limitations it is impossible to explain the complete semantic setup, but the interested reader is referred to Copestake, Flickinger, Pollard & Sag (2005).[3]

(91) Lexical entry for the stem *geb-* 'give':

$$\begin{bmatrix} \text{ARG-ST} & \left\langle \text{NP}[str]_{\boxed{1}}, \text{NP}[ldat]_{\boxed{2}}, \text{NP}[str]_{\boxed{3}} \right\rangle \\ \text{CONT} & \begin{bmatrix} \text{IND} & \boxed{4}\ event \end{bmatrix} \\ \text{RELS} & \left\langle \begin{bmatrix} geben & \\ \text{ARG0} & \boxed{4} \\ \text{ARG1} & \boxed{1} \\ \text{ARG2} & \boxed{2} \\ \text{ARG3} & \boxed{3} \end{bmatrix} \right\rangle \end{bmatrix}$$

The linking pattern for the English lexical item is completely parallel: the first argument is linked to ARG1, the second to ARG2, and the third to ARG3.

This seems to be similar to what Asudeh et al. (2014) do with their AGENT and PATIENT templates. The AGENT template introduces an ARG_1 and the PATIENT template introduces an ARG_2. See page 12 for the definition of their templates. For the predicate *draw* they assume that it has an ARG_1 and an ARG_2 on semantic structure if it is used without the benefactive argument. The benefactive template adds an ARG_3 and remaps ARG_2 to ARG_3. So rather than *godzilla*, abbreviated as g in (92a), *Sandy* is the ARG_2 in (92b). *Godzilla* is ARG_3 in (92b).

(92) a. s-structure for *Kim drew godzilla*:

$$\begin{bmatrix} \text{REL} & draw \\ \text{EVENT} & ev \\ \text{ARG1} & k \\ \text{ARG2} & g \end{bmatrix}$$

b. s-structure for *Kim drew Sandy godzilla*:

$$\begin{bmatrix} \text{REL} & draw \\ \text{EVENT} & ev \\ \text{ARG1} & k \\ \text{ARG2} & s \\ \text{ARG3} & g \end{bmatrix}$$

[3] The representations below are simplified. I do not use handles and labels as is common in Minimal Recursion Semantics.

This is different in the HPSG proposal. The type definition states that *draw* has an event variable (ARG0) and two arguments (ARG1, ARG2). The benefactive cannot be added to the structure of *drew* since the definition of the transitive verb *draw* does not contain a slot for a benefactive argument. As will be shown below the information about the benefactive relation is introduced in a Neo-Davidsonian way instead.

7.2.3 Lexical rules

This section discusses the lexical rules for benefactives and for resultative constructions and the interaction of these lexical rules with nominalization.

7.2.3.1 Benefactives

I assume the lexical rule in (93) for adding an additional benefactive argument:

(93) Lexical rule for benefactives (German and English):

$$\begin{bmatrix} \textit{stem} \\ \text{ARG-ST} & \left\langle \boxed{1}\ \text{NP}[\textit{str}] \right\rangle \oplus \boxed{2} \left\langle \text{NP}[\textit{str}] \mid \ldots \right\rangle \\ \text{CONT} & \begin{bmatrix} \text{IND} & \boxed{3} \end{bmatrix} \\ \text{RELS} & \boxed{4} \end{bmatrix} \mapsto$$

$$\begin{bmatrix} \text{ARG-ST} & \left\langle \boxed{1}\ \text{NP}[\textit{str}], \text{NP}_{\boxed{5}} \right\rangle \oplus \boxed{2} \\ \text{CONT} & \begin{bmatrix} \text{IND} & \boxed{3} \end{bmatrix} \\ \text{RELS} & \boxed{4} \oplus \left\langle \begin{bmatrix} \textit{benefactive} \\ \text{ARG0} & \boxed{3} \\ \text{ARG1} & \boxed{5} \end{bmatrix} \right\rangle \end{bmatrix}$$

The ARG-ST list of the input has to include two NPs with structural case (a nominative and an accusative argument in the active). The ARG-ST list of the input is split into two lists: one that contains a single NP[*str*] and another one that contains an NP[*str*] and some possibly non-empty rest. The ARG-ST in the output of the lexical rule contains the initial NP of the input ($\boxed{1}$), an additional NP and the list $\boxed{2}$, that is, at least the second NP with structural case. The input description mentions the index of the input verb, which is the event variable ($\boxed{3}$). The list of semantic relations that is contributed by the input sign is $\boxed{4}$. The output specification of the lexical rule contains the list of relations of the input plus a benefactive relation that states that the benefactive of the event $\boxed{3}$ is $\boxed{5}$. $\boxed{5}$ is identified with the referential index of the added NP.

The output of the lexical rule is a verb stem with at least three arguments. Language-specific constraints for verbs with three nominal arguments apply and ensure that the middle NP has structural case in English and lexical dative in German. This is not shown in the general version of the lexical rule above. The English version of the rule is more restrictive than the German one in requiring that the input be strictly transitive. This excludes the application of the benefactive lexical rule to the output of the resultative lexical rule for English but allows for this in German.

The result of applying the lexical rule to (94a) is (94b):

(94) a. monotransitive version of *backen*:

$$\begin{bmatrix} \text{PHON} & \left\langle \textit{back} \right\rangle \\ \text{ARG-ST} & \left\langle \text{NP}[\textit{str}]_{\boxed{1}}, \text{NP}[\textit{str}]_{\boxed{2}} \right\rangle \\ \text{IND} & \boxed{3}\ \textit{event} \\ \text{RELS} & \left\langle \begin{bmatrix} \textit{backen} & \\ \text{ARG0} & \boxed{3} \\ \text{ARG1} & \boxed{1} \\ \text{ARG2} & \boxed{2} \end{bmatrix} \right\rangle \end{bmatrix}$$

b. ditransitive version of *backen*:

$$\begin{bmatrix} \text{PHON} & \left\langle \textit{back} \right\rangle \\ \text{ARG-ST} & \left\langle \text{NP}[\textit{str}]_{\boxed{1}}, \text{NP}[\textit{ldat}]_{\boxed{4}}, \text{NP}[\textit{str}]_{\boxed{2}} \right\rangle \\ \text{IND} & \boxed{3}\ \textit{event} \\ \text{RELS} & \left\langle \begin{bmatrix} \textit{backen} & \\ \text{ARG0} & \boxed{3} \\ \text{ARG1} & \boxed{1} \\ \text{ARG2} & \boxed{2} \end{bmatrix}, \begin{bmatrix} \textit{benefactive} & \\ \text{ARG0} & \boxed{3} \\ \text{ARG1} & \boxed{4} \end{bmatrix} \right\rangle \end{bmatrix}$$

A dative argument is added between the two NPs that bear structural case and this dative argument is linked to a role in the benefactive relation.

The lexical item for the three-place *bake* in English would be parallel to (94b). Since this *bake* has the same valency as the three-place verb *give*, the syntactic structure it can appear in is parallel. See Figure 7.1 for an example.

Of course, the analysis presented here is incomplete in the sense that further constraints are needed to prevent the application of the rule to semantically inappropriate verbs. Since the focus of the book is to discuss phrasal and lexical approaches and since the incorporation of the respective semantic constraints into a phrasal approach would be exactly parallel, I do not go into semantic details here.

7.2.3.2 Resultative constructions

The lexical rule for resultative constructions with intransitive, mono-valent verbs or mono-valent variants of transitive verbs is provided in (95):[4]

(95) Lexical rule for resultatives:

$$\begin{bmatrix} \textsc{arg-st} & \left\langle \boxed{1}\ \text{NP}[str] \right\rangle \\ \textsc{cont} & \begin{bmatrix} \textsc{ind}\ \boxed{2} \end{bmatrix} \\ \textsc{rels} & \boxed{3} \end{bmatrix} \mapsto$$

$$\begin{bmatrix} \textsc{arg-st} & \left\langle \boxed{1}, \boxed{4}\ \text{NP}[str], \text{X(P)}[\textsc{prd}+, \textsc{subj}\ \langle\ \boxed{4}\ \rangle]{:}\boxed{5} \right\rangle \\ \textsc{cont} & \begin{bmatrix} \textsc{ind}\ \boxed{6}\ event \end{bmatrix} \\ \textsc{rels} & \boxed{3} \oplus \left\langle \begin{bmatrix} cause \\ \textsc{arg0}\ \boxed{6} \\ \textsc{arg1}\ \boxed{2} \\ \textsc{arg2}\ \boxed{7} \end{bmatrix}, \begin{bmatrix} become \\ \textsc{arg0}\ \boxed{7} \\ \textsc{arg1}\ \boxed{5} \end{bmatrix} \right\rangle \end{bmatrix}$$

The input is a verbal stem that selects for an NP with structural case and the output is a verbal stem selecting for two NPs with structural case and a result predicate. The second NP is both an argument of the verb and the subject of the result predicate. I assume that there is not a person that causes the change of state but rather that the event of the input verb ($\boxed{2}$) causes the change of state. This makes it possible to capture cases in which there is no participant in the causing event:[5]

(96) Es regnet die Stühle / Wäsche nass.
it rains the chairs clothes wet

The highest event of the semantic representation in the output of the rule is the *cause* event ($\boxed{6}$). Since *cause* is the highest event, $\boxed{6}$ is also the INDEX value of the output, which is represented under CONT|IND. The *cause* event has as its first argument the event expressed by the input verb ($\boxed{2}$) and as its second argument the *become* predicate ($\boxed{7}$). The *become* predicate takes the contribution of the predicative phrase ($\boxed{5}$) as its argument.

[4]This rule is not complete. Further constraints regarding the semantics of the input verb have to be stated.

[5]Parallel structures in English are ungrammatical. They can be ruled out by requiring that the first NP argument is referential.

The result of the rule application to (97a) is shown in (97b):

(97) a. intransitive version of *fischen*:

$$\begin{bmatrix} \text{PHON} & \langle \textit{fisch} \rangle \\ \text{ARG-ST} & \langle \text{NP}[\textit{str}]_{\boxed{1}} \rangle \\ \text{IND} & \boxed{6} \\ \text{RELS} & \left\langle \begin{bmatrix} \textit{fischen} & \\ \text{ARG0} & \boxed{6} \\ \text{ARG1} & \boxed{1} \end{bmatrix} \right\rangle \end{bmatrix}$$

b. resultative version of *fischen*:

$$\begin{bmatrix} \text{PHON} & \langle \textit{fisch} \rangle \\ \text{ARG-ST} & \langle \text{NP}[\textit{str}]_{\boxed{1}}, \boxed{2}\ \text{NP}[\textit{str}], \text{X(P)}[\text{PRD+}, \text{SUBJ}\ \langle \boxed{2} \rangle]{:}\boxed{4} \rangle \\ \text{IND} & \boxed{5} \\ \text{RELS} & \left\langle \begin{bmatrix} \textit{fischen} & \\ \text{ARG0} & \boxed{6} \\ \text{ARG1} & \boxed{1} \end{bmatrix}, \begin{bmatrix} \textit{cause} & \\ \text{ARG0} & \boxed{5} \\ \text{ARG1} & \boxed{6} \\ \text{ARG2} & \boxed{7} \end{bmatrix}, \begin{bmatrix} \textit{become} & \\ \text{ARG0} & \boxed{7} \\ \text{ARG1} & \boxed{4} \end{bmatrix} \right\rangle \end{bmatrix}$$

The event variable of the *cause* relation is $\boxed{5}$. It is also the IND value of the lexical item. $\boxed{6}$ is the event variable of *fischen*. It is the ARG1 of the *cause* relation. The second argument of the *cause* relation is the *become* relation. The *become* relation takes the semantic contribution of the result predicate ($\boxed{4}$) as argument.

A more readable semantic representation corresponding to the one in (97b) is given in (98):

(98) cause(e1, fischen(e2,x), become(e3,P))

The lexical item for the resultative construction may be input to the benefactive lexical rule. The output is shown in (99):

(99) ditransitive version of resultative *fischen*:

$$\begin{bmatrix} \text{PHON} & \langle \textit{fisch} \rangle \\ \text{ARG-ST} & \langle \text{NP}[\textit{str}]_{\boxed{1}}, \text{NP}[\textit{ldat}]_{\boxed{3}}, \boxed{2}\ \text{NP}[\textit{str}], \text{X(P)}[\text{PRD+}, \text{SUBJ}\ \langle \boxed{2} \rangle]{:}\boxed{4} \rangle \\ \text{IND} & \boxed{5} \\ \text{RELS} & \left\langle \begin{bmatrix} \textit{fischen} & \\ \text{ARG0} & \boxed{6} \\ \text{ARG1} & \boxed{1} \end{bmatrix}, \begin{bmatrix} \textit{cause} & \\ \text{ARG0} & \boxed{5} \\ \text{ARG1} & \boxed{6} \\ \text{ARG2} & \boxed{7} \end{bmatrix}, \begin{bmatrix} \textit{become} & \\ \text{ARG0} & \boxed{7} \\ \text{ARG1} & \boxed{4} \end{bmatrix}, \begin{bmatrix} \textit{benefactive} & \\ \text{ARG0} & \boxed{5} \\ \text{ARG1} & \boxed{3} \end{bmatrix} \right\rangle \end{bmatrix}$$

In (99) we have NP[*str*], NP[*str*] and the predicative X(P) as arguments and in addition we also have the benefactive NP[*ldat*]. The benefactive NP is linked to the *benefactive* relation (3).

A more readable semantic representation corresponding to (99) is the formula in (100):

(100) cause(e1, fischen(e2,x), become(e3,P)) ∧ benefactive(e1,y)

Figure 7.6 shows the analysis of (85c). The resultative lexical rule applies to the mono-valent version of the lexical item for *fish-* 'to fish'. The lexical rule licenses

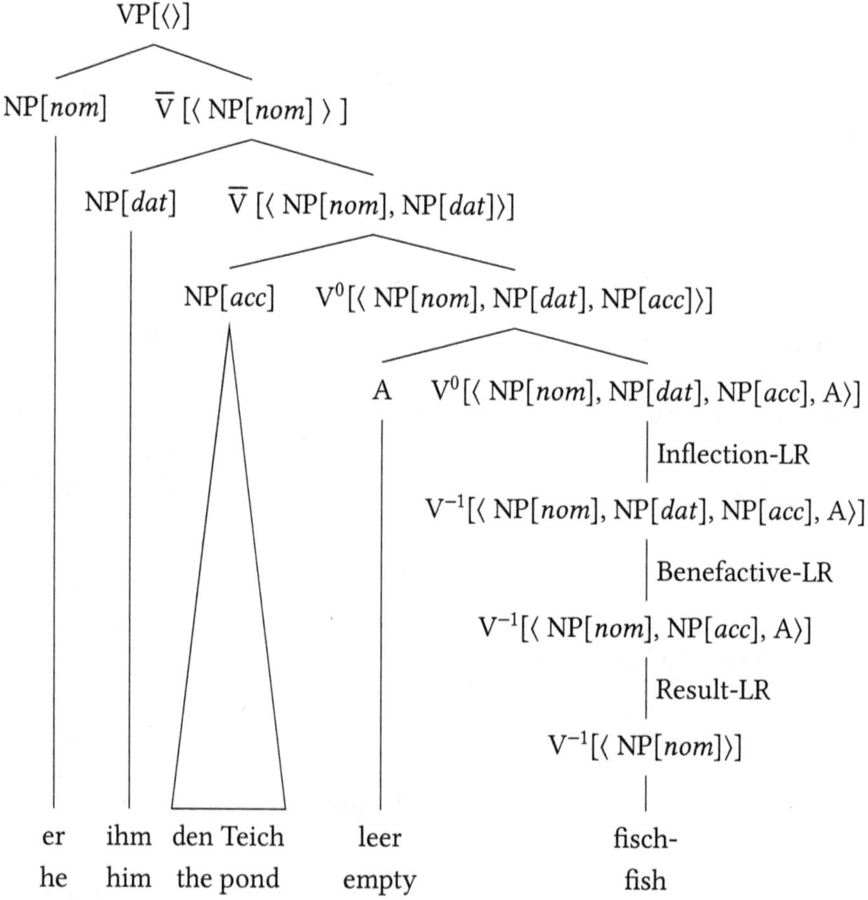

Figure 7.6: Analysis of [*dass*] *er ihm den Teich leer fischt* 'that he fishes the pond empty for him', an example in which the benefactive and the resultative construction interact

another stem that selects for two NPs with structural case, which are resolved to nominative and accusative in the example at hand. The benefactive lexical rule applies to this lexical item and licenses another lexical item that selects for nominative, dative, accusative and a result predicate. An inflectional lexical rule licenses the V^0. The V^0 is combined with the adjective to form a verbal complex, indicated by the label V^0 at the mother node. *leer fischt* is combined with its arguments by the German version of the Head-Complement Schema in Figure 7.5, and hence it is explained why six orders of the nominative, dative and accusative argument are possible. In the analysis suggested here, the fact that scrambling is possible is a fact of German syntax that is independent of how the arguments are licensed.

Note that all the stems in Figure 7.6 could be input to derivational lexical rules that derive prenominal participles:

(101) a. der fischende Mann
the fishing man

b. der den Teich leer fischende Mann
the the pond empty fishing man
'the man who fishes the pond empty'

c. der den Teich seinem Freund leer fischende Mann
the the pond his friend empty fishing man
'the man who fishes the pond empty for his friend'

d. der leer gefischte Teich
the empty fished pond

e. der dem Besitzer leer gefischte Teich
the the owner empty fished pond
'the pond that was fished empty for the owner'

The derivational rules are independent of the benefactive and the resultative construction and apply to verbs that have a subject in the case of the first participle formed with *-end* and to verbs that have an underlying object (transitive verbs and unaccusative ones) in the case of the second participle formed with *ge- -t*. See Müller (2002: 160) for a formulation of the latter rule.

7.2.3.3 Nominalizations

There are several variants of nominalizations. The noun can be used with an agent as specifier as in (102a) or with a normal determiner as in (102b,c):

(102) a. Peters Leerfischung des Teiches
Peter's empty.fishing of.the pond

b. die Leerfischung des Teiches
the empty.fishing of.the pond

c. die Leerfischung des Teiches durch Peter
the empty.fishing of.the pond by Peter

The important point is that this is independent of the resultative construction. (103) shows an example with a transitive verb:

(103) a. Peters Zerstörung des Buches
Peter's destruction of.the book

b. die Zerstörung des Buches
the destruction of.the book

c. die Zerstörung des Buches durch Peter
the destruction of.the book by Peter

I assume that the nominalization attaches to the verb stem. In the case of the resultative construction in (102) the result predicate is then combined with the derived nominal stem. As the result of the combination we get a word that has one or more NPs with structural case on its ARG-ST list. The case principle assigns genitive to these NPs since it is realized in a nominal environment.

7.3 Constraints on extraction and passivization

Toivonen (2013: 516) argues that the benefactive construction is best seen as an instantiation of the phrasal configuration in Figure 1.4 on page 9. She noticed that question formation involving the extraction of the benefactive NP is excluded. The respective examples in (7) are repeated here as (104) and (105) for convenience:

(104) a. I baked Linda cookies

b. * Who did I bake cookies?

(105) a. The kids drew their teacher a picture.

b. * Which teacher did the kids draw a picture?

She also discusses the example in (8) – repeated as (106) – , which is judged ungrammatical by speakers of certain dialects of English:

(106) * My sister was carved a soap statue of Bugs Bunny (by a famous sculptor).

She observed that all these ungrammatical examples are accounted for by assuming that benefactives are licensed in structures like the one given in Figure 1.4.

If one wanted to assume that a certain configuration is stored as chunk, one could do so without problems in the model suggested here. Figure 7.7 shows what would be stored for English. The figure shows a chunk and of course cer-

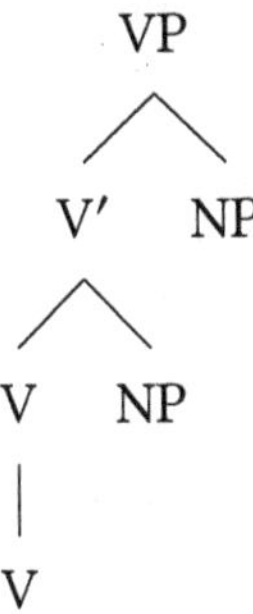

Figure 7.7: Stored phrasal configuration for English

tain slots in this structure can be filled. The important point about the figure is that the lexical rule application that maps a two-place verb to a three-place one would be part of the stored configuration. This ensures that language-internal and crosslinguistic generalizations are captured. However, as I have shown, storing a phrasal configuration is not what is required here since extraction of the secondary object is possible (42) and the construction may be realized discontinuously in coordination structures (58). However, there are other ways of blocking extraction and passivization. The passive is treated as the suppression of the subject. If there is an object with structural case, it is the least oblique element in the passive and therefore it gets nominative by the Case Principle, which is usually assumed. Now, if the case of the object is lexically constrained to be accusative, the verbal lexeme can only be used in the active since otherwise the case specification of the benefactive argument as accusative would be in conflict with the assignment of nominative by the Case Principle. So, for speakers that allow for passivization, the case of the subject and the two objects is just specified as structural with the actual value being underspecified, and for speakers who do not allow for a passive, the case of the benefactive argument is specified to be accusative.

The extraction of primary objects is marked for all verbs that take two objects irrespective of the semantic role. For some speakers the extraction of benefactives is worse than the extraction of other primary objects. If one wanted to block extraction via a hard constraint rather than assuming that performance factors play a role here (Langendoen et al. 1973), one could state that the SLASH value of the primary object is the empty list (Müller 1999: 98) or – if extraction out of the primary object is to be permitted – different from the LOCAL value of the primary object. Because of this specification a trace would be incompatible with this object. The same applies to an appropriately specified lexical rule for argument extraction (Müller 1996: 226) or a process like SLASH amalgamation as suggested by Bouma, Malouf & Sag (2001).

Note that this approach also predicts that constraints on extraction and passivization in coordinated structures affect the result of coordination. The reason is that the constraints on the selected arguments are identified in symmetric coordinations (Pollard & Sag 1994: 202). Hence, the SLASH constraints and the case constraints on the benefactive argument are effective on the mother node of verb coordinations as well. So, the analyses that introduce constraints for extraction and passivization lexically correctly predict that the coordination of two items is at least as restrictive as the individual conjuncts, while in approaches that introduce the constraints on the phrasal level, coordinating items may result in an object that can enter less restrictive phrasal rules.

For completeness it should be noted that the German benefactive construction is much less restricted. The benefactive arguments can be extracted in German and can be used in questions:

(107) a. Wem habe ich Kekse gebacken?
who.DAT have I.NOM cookies.ACC baked

b. Welchem Lehrer haben die Kinder ein Bild gemalt?
which.DAT teacher have the.NOM children a.ACC picture drawn

As (67) shows, the construction also interacts with the dative passive. Hence, Toivonen's original motivation for a phrasal approach would not apply to German.

Since I have shown how the respective constraints can be formulated in a lexical approach, there is now a proposal that captures both German and English and the commonalities between the two languages.

8 Conclusions

I have shown that both the benefactive and the resultative construction are more flexible than originally suggested by the authors who proposed phrasal configurations. All non-verbal parts of the resultative construction may be extracted or promoted by passivization. The secondary object of benefactive constructions may be extracted and some speakers allow for passivization.

I have also shown that morphology needs access to valence (adjective formation and *-bar* 'able' derivation). Alsina (1996) showed that a lexical analysis of the passive is possible even for analyses that introduce the accusative object syntactically. But the examples that were discussed in the present book involved the selection of lexemes governing an accusative in the morphology component. If this valence information is not added to lexical items but dependents are introduced by phrasal constructions instead, there is no way to account for the insights regarding morphological rules.

Furthermore, I have argued that either the c-structure does not add any constraints in a template-based phrasal approach or the relation between active and passive variants of a construction is not covered. I also showed that the phrasal analysis of English benefactive and resultative constructions does not carry over to languages that are assumed to have different c-structures. As was the case for the phrasal GPSG approach to valence, partial phrases that play a role in coordination, partial fronting, and also certain accounts of fronting are problematic for pattern-based approaches to argument structure.

I have shown that all these problems disappear and crosslinguistic generalizations regarding the benefactive, resultative and many other constructions can be captured if one returns to the traditional lexical analysis, which assumed that all arguments are introduced lexically. A version of the lexical analysis was presented in Chapter 7. This analysis is the basis of implemented fragments of German and English that have been developed in the CoreGram project (Müller 2007c; 2015b). As was demonstrated, the lexical rule for the benefactive in German and English is the same. The languages differ in how the second argument of ditransitive verbs is realized since German has a morphologically marked dative case, which is absent from English. But this is a general property of ditransitive verbs that is independent of the benefactive rule. Lexical rules for resultative predicates are parallel for English and German. The differences are due to the differences in the syntactic systems of the languages but this is independent of the resultative construction.

With the system of lexical rules in place, the phrasal schemata for specifier-head structures and head-complement structures in German and English are identical (or rather the schema for English is a specialization of the one for German). No special construction-specific stipulations are needed.

By having shown that approaches assuming the resultative construction and/or the benefactive construction to be phrasal constructions run into problems, I have also shown that approaches considering all argument structure constructions phrasal are problematic. Hence, this book is a contribution to the general debate about argument structure constructions. It shows that phrasal constructions (in LFG) are not suited to deal with argument structure. Instead, lexical constructions (lexical rules) are needed. The syntactic combinations are licensed by rather abstract syntactic rules. Nevertheless, phrasal constructions are useful and necessary in those parts of grammars that do not interact with argument structure and valence alternations. An example of such a construction is the N-P-N construction (*student after student*), in which no head can be identified (Jackendoff 2008). So, this book provides support for the position that a mix of the proposals from the two major linguistic schools is needed: we need a rich lexicon and abstract schemata for combining linguistic objects and we need specific phrasal constructions that contribute their own semantics.

References

Abney, Steven P. 1996. Statistical methods and linguistics. In Judith L. Klavans & Philip Resnik (eds.), *The balancing act: combining symbolic and statistical approaches to language* (Language, Speech, and Communication), 1–26. London, England/Cambridge, MA: MIT Press.

Ackerman, Farrell & Gert Webelhuth. 1998. *A theory of predicates* (CSLI Lecture Notes 76). Stanford, CA: CSLI Publications.

Adger, David. 2003. *Core syntax: A Minimalist approach* (Oxford Core Linguistics 1). Oxford: Oxford University Press.

Alsina, Alex. 1996. Resultatives: A joint operation of semantic and syntactic structures. In Miriam Butt & Tracy Holloway King (eds.), *Proceedings of the LFG '96 conference, Rank Xerox, Grenoble.* Stanford, CA: CSLI Publications. http://csli-publications.stanford.edu/LFG/1/, accessed 2018-02-25.

Asudeh, Ash, Mary Dalrymple & Ida Toivonen. 2008. Constructions with lexical integrity: Templates as the lexicon-syntax interface. In Miriam Butt & Tracy Holloway King (eds.), *Proceedings of the LFG 2008 conference.* Stanford, CA: CSLI Publications. http://csli-publications.stanford.edu/LFG/13/, accessed 2018-02-25.

Asudeh, Ash, Mary Dalrymple & Ida Toivonen. 2013. Constructions with lexical integrity. *Journal of Language Modelling* 1(1). 1–54.

Asudeh, Ash, Gianluca Giorgolo & Ida Toivonen. 2014. Meaning and valency. In Miriam Butt & Tracy Holloway King (eds.), *Proceedings of the LFG 2014 conference*, 68–88. Stanford, CA: CSLI Publications.

Asudeh, Ash & Ida Toivonen. 2014. *With* lexical integrity. *Theoretical Linguistics* 40(1–2). 175–186.

Bech, Gunnar. 1955. *Studien über das deutsche Verbum infinitum* (Linguistische Arbeiten 139). Tübingen: Max Niemeyer Verlag. 2nd unchanged edition 1983.

Bergen, Benjamin K. & Nancy Chang. 2005. Embodied Construction Grammar in simulation-based language understanding. In Jan-Ola Östman & Mirjam Fried (eds.), *Construction Grammars: Cognitive grounding and theoretical extensions*, 147–190. Amsterdam: John Benjamins Publishing Co.

Berman, Judith. 1996. Eine LFG-Grammatik des Deutschen. In *Deutsche und französische Syntax im Formalismus der LFG* (Linguistische Arbeiten 344), 11–96. Tübingen: Max Niemeyer Verlag.

Berman, Judith. 2003. *Clausal syntax of German* (Studies in Constraint-Based Lexicalism). Stanford, CA: CSLI Publications.

Blevins, James P. 2003. Passives and impersonals. *Journal of Linguistics* 39(3). 473–520.

Bloom, Paul. 1993. Grammatical continuity in language development: The case of subjectless sentences. *Linguistic Inquiry* 24(4). 721–734.

Bod, Rens. 2009. From exemplar to grammar: Integrating analogy and probability in language learning. *Cognitive Science* 33(4). 752–793.

Bouma, Gosse, Robert Malouf & Ivan A. Sag. 2001. Satisfying constraints on extraction and adjunction. *Natural Language and Linguistic Theory* 19(1). 1–65.

Bouma, Gosse & Gertjan van Noord. 1998. Word order constraints on verb clusters in German and Dutch. In Erhard W. Hinrichs, Andreas Kathol & Tsuneko Nakazawa (eds.), *Complex predicates in nonderivational syntax* (Syntax and Semantics 30), 43–72. San Diego: Academic Press.

Bresnan, Joan. 1978. A realistic Transformational Grammar. In Morris Halle, Joan Bresnan & George A. Miller (eds.), *Linguistic theory and psychological reality*, 1–59. Cambridge, MA: MIT Press.

Bresnan, Joan. 1982. The passive in lexical theory. In Joan Bresnan (ed.), *The mental representation of grammatical relations* (MIT Press Series on Cognitive Theory and Mental Representation), 3–86. Cambridge, MA/London: MIT Press.

Bresnan, Joan. 2001. *Lexical-Functional Syntax*. Oxford: Blackwell Publishers Ltd.

Bresnan, Joan, Ash Asudeh, Ida Toivonen & Stephen Mark Wechsler. 2015. *Lexical-functional syntax*. 2nd edn. Oxford: Blackwell Publishers Ltd. DOI:10.1002/9781119105664

Bresnan, Joan & Jonni M. Kanerva. 1989. Locative inversion in Chichewa: A case study of factorization in grammar. *Linguistic Inquiry* 20(1). 1–50.

Bresnan, Joan, Ronald M. Kaplan, Stanley Peters & Annie Zaenen. 1982. Cross-serial dependencies in Dutch. *Linguistic Inquiry* 13(4). 613–635.

Bresnan, Joan & Annie Zaenen. 1990. Deep unaccusativity in LFG. In Katarzyna Dziwirek, Patrick Farrell & Errapel Mejías-Bikandi (eds.), *Grammatical relations: A cross-theoretical perspective*, 45–57. Stanford, CA: CSLI Publications.

Briscoe, Ted J. & Ann Copestake. 1999. Lexical rules in constraint-based grammar. *Computational Linguistics* 25(4). 487–526. http://www.aclweb.org/anthology/J99-4002, accessed 2018-10-07.

Bruening, Benjamin. 2018. The lexicalist hypothesis: Both wrong and superfluous. *Language* 94(1). 1–42. DOI:10.1353/lan.2018.0000

Cappelle, Bert. 2006. Particle placement and the case for "allostructions". *Constructions online* 1(7). 1–28.

Carrier, Jill & Janet H. Randall. 1992. The argument structure and syntactic structure of resultatives. *Linguistic Inquiry* 23(2). 173–234.

Choi, Hye-Won. 1999. *Optimizing structure in scrambling: Scrambling and information structure* (Dissertations in Linguistics). Stanford, CA: CSLI Publications.

Chomsky, Noam. 1957. *Syntactic structures* (Janua Linguarum / Series Minor 4). The Hague/Paris: Mouton.

Chomsky, Noam. 1973. Conditions on transformations. In Stephen R. Anderson & Paul Kiparsky (eds.), *A festschrift for Morris Halle*, 232–286. New York: Holt, Rinehart & Winston.

Chomsky, Noam. 1981. *Lectures on government and binding*. Dordrecht: Foris Publications.

Chomsky, Noam. 1995. *The Minimalist Program* (Current Studies in Linguistics 28). Cambridge, MA: MIT Press.

Chomsky, Noam. 2001. *Beyond explanatory adequacy*. Cambridge, MA: MIT Press.

Christie, Elizabeth. 2010. Using templates to account for English resultatives. In Miriam Butt & Tracy Holloway King (eds.), *Proceedings of the LFG 2010 conference*, 155–164. Stanford, CA: CSLI Publications. http://csli-publications.stanford.edu/LFG/15/, accessed 2018-03-20.

Christie, Elizabeth. 2015. *The English resultative*. Carleton University Ottawa, Ontario dissertation.

Cook, Philippa. 2006. The datives that aren't born equal: Beneficiaries and the dative passive. In Daniel Hole, André Meinunger & Werner Abraham (eds.), *Datives and similar cases: Between argument structure and event structure*, 141–184. Amsterdam: John Benjamins Publishing Co.

Copestake, Ann, Daniel P. Flickinger, Carl J. Pollard & Ivan A. Sag. 2005. Minimal Recursion Semantics: An introduction. *Research on Language and Computation* 3(2–3). 281–332. DOI:10.1007/s11168-006-6327-9

Croft, William. 2001. *Radical Construction Grammar: Syntactic theory in typological perspective*. Oxford: Oxford University Press.

Croft, William. 2003. Lexical rules vs. constructions: A false dichotomy. In Hubert Cuyckens, Thomas Berg, René Dirven & Klaus-Uwe Panther (eds.), *Motivation in language: Studies in honour of Günter Radden* (Current Issues in

Linguistic Theory 243), 49–68. Amsterdam: John Benjamins Publishing Co. DOI:10.1075/cilt.243.07cro

Culicover, Peter W. & Ray S. Jackendoff. 2005. *Simpler Syntax*. Oxford: Oxford University Press.

Dalrymple, Mary (ed.). 1999. *Semantics and syntax in Lexical Functional Grammar: The Resource Logic approach* (Language, Speech, and Communication). Cambridge, MA: MIT Press.

Dalrymple, Mary. 2001. *Lexical Functional Grammar* (Syntax and Semantics 34). New York, NY: Academic Press.

Dalrymple, Mary, Ronald M. Kaplan & Tracy Holloway King. 2001. Weak crossover and the absence of traces. In Miriam Butt & Tracy Holloway King (eds.), *Proceedings of the LFG 2001 conference*, 66–82. Stanford, CA: CSLI Publications. http://csli-publications.stanford.edu/LFG/6/, accessed 2018-02-25.

Dalrymple, Mary, Ronald M. Kaplan & Tracy Holloway King. 2004. Linguistic generalizations over descriptions. In Miriam Butt & Tracy Holloway King (eds.), *Proceedings of the LFG 2004 conference*, 199–208. Stanford, CA: CSLI Publications. http://csli-publications.stanford.edu/LFG/9/, accessed 2018-02-25.

Davis, Anthony R. & Jean-Pierre Koenig. 2000. Linking as constraints on word classes in a hierarchical lexicon. *Language* 76(1). 56–91.

Dowty, David R. 1978. Governed transformations as lexical rules in a Montague Grammar. *Linguistic Inquiry* 9(3). 393–426.

Eisenberg, Peter. 1994. German. In Ekkehard König & Johan van der Auwera (eds.), *The Germanic languages* (Routledge Language Family Descriptions), 349–387. London: Routledge.

Fillmore, Charles J., Paul Kay & Mary Catherine O'Connor. 1988. Regularity and idiomaticity in grammatical constructions: The case of *let alone*. *Language* 64(3). 501–538.

Findlay, Jamie Y. 2016. Mapping theory without argument structure. *Journal of Language Modelling* 4(2). 293–338.

Forst, Martin & Christian Rohrer. 2009. Problems of German VP coordination. In Miriam Butt & Tracy Holloway King (eds.), *Proceedings of the LFG 2009 conference*, 297–316. Stanford, CA: CSLI Publications. http://csli-publications.stanford.edu/LFG/14/, accessed 2018-02-25.

Freudenthal, Daniel, Julian M. Pine, Javier Aguado-Orea & Fernand Gobet. 2007. Modeling the developmental patterning of finiteness marking in English, Dutch, German, and Spanish using MOSAIC. *Cognitive Science* 31(2). 311–341. DOI:10.1080/15326900701221454

Gazdar, Gerald, Ewan Klein, Geoffrey K. Pullum & Ivan A. Sag. 1985. *Generalized Phrase Structure Grammar*. Cambridge, MA: Harvard University Press.

Goldberg, Adele E. 1991. A semantic account of resultatives. *Linguistic Analysis* 21(1–2). 66–96.

Goldberg, Adele E. 1995. *Constructions: A Construction Grammar approach to argument structure* (Cognitive Theory of Language and Culture). Chicago/London: The University of Chicago Press.

Goldberg, Adele E. 2004. But do we need Universal Grammar? Comment on Lidz et al. (2003). *Cognition* 94(1). 77–84. DOI:10.1016/j.cognition.2004.03.003

Goldberg, Adele E. 2006. *Constructions at work: The nature of generalization in language* (Oxford Linguistics). Oxford: Oxford University Press.

Goldberg, Adele E. 2013a. Argument structure Constructions vs. lexical rules or derivational verb templates. *Mind and Language* 28(4). 435–465. DOI:10.1111/mila.12026

Goldberg, Adele E. 2013b. Explanation and Constructions: Response to Adger. *Mind and Language* 28(4). 479–491. DOI:10.1111/mila.12028

Goldberg, Adele E. & Ray S. Jackendoff. 2004. The English resultative as a family of Constructions. *Language* 80(3). 532–568.

Haider, Hubert. 1986. Fehlende Argumente: Vom Passiv zu kohärenten Infinitiven. *Linguistische Berichte* 101. 3–33.

Haider, Hubert. 1990. Topicalization and other puzzles of German syntax. In Günther Grewendorf & Wolfgang Sternefeld (eds.), *Scrambling and Barriers* (Linguistik Aktuell/Linguistics Today 5), 93–112. Amsterdam: John Benjamins Publishing Co. DOI:10.1075/la.5.06hai

Haider, Hubert. 1993. *Deutsche Syntax – generativ: Vorstudien zur Theorie einer projektiven Grammatik* (Tübinger Beiträge zur Linguistik 325). Tübingen: Gunter Narr Verlag.

Haider, Hubert. 1994. (Un-)heimliche Subjekte: Anmerkungen zur Pro-drop Causa, im Anschluß an die Lektüre von Osvaldo Jaeggli & Kenneth J. Safir, eds., The Null Subject Parameter. *Linguistische Berichte* 153. 372–385.

Haider, Hubert. 2001. Parametrisierung in der Generativen Grammatik. In Martin Haspelmath, Ekkehard König, Wulf Oesterreicher & Wolfgang Raible (eds.), *Sprachtypologie und sprachliche Universalien – Language typology and language universals: Ein internationales Handbuch – An international handbook*, 283–294. Berlin: Mouton de Gruyter.

Haugereid, Petter. 2007. Decomposed phrasal constructions. In Stefan Müller (ed.), *Proceedings of the 14th International Conference on Head-Driven Phrase*

Structure Grammar, 120–129. Stanford, CA: CSLI Publications. http://csli-publications.stanford.edu/HPSG/2007/, accessed 2018-02-25.

Haugereid, Petter. 2009. *Phrasal subconstructions: A Constructionalist grammar design, exemplified with Norwegian and English.* Norwegian University of Science & Technology, Trondheim dissertation.

Hauser, Marc D., Noam Chomsky & W. Tecumseh Fitch. 2002. The faculty of language: What is it, who has it, and how did it evolve? *Science* 298(5598). 1569–1579. DOI:10.1126/science.298.5598.1569

Hinrichs, Erhard W. & Tsuneko Nakazawa. 1989. Subcategorization and VP structure in German. In *Aspects of German VP structure* (SfS-Report-01-93). Tübingen: Eberhard-Karls-Universität Tübingen.

Hinrichs, Erhard W. & Tsuneko Nakazawa. 1994. Linearizing AUXs in German verbal complexes. In John Nerbonne, Klaus Netter & Carl J. Pollard (eds.), *German in Head-Driven Phrase Structure Grammar* (CSLI Lecture Notes 46), 11–38. Stanford, CA: CSLI Publications.

Hudson, Richard. 1992. So-called 'double objects' and grammatical relations. *Language* 68(2). 251–276.

Jackendoff, Ray S. 1977. *$\overline{X}$ syntax: A study of phrase structure.* Cambridge, MA: MIT Press.

Jackendoff, Ray S. 2008. Construction after Construction and its theoretical challenges. *Language* 84(1). 8–28.

Johnson, Mark. 1986. A GPSG account of VP structure in German. *Linguistics* 24(5). 871–882.

Kaplan, Ronald M. & Annie Zaenen. 1989. Long-distance dependencies, constituent structure and functional uncertainty. In Mark R. Baltin & Anthony S. Kroch (eds.), *Alternative conceptions of phrase structure*, 17–42. Chicago/London: The University of Chicago Press.

Kasper, Robert T. 1994. Adjuncts in the Mittelfeld. In John Nerbonne, Klaus Netter & Carl J. Pollard (eds.), *German in Head-Driven Phrase Structure Grammar* (CSLI Lecture Notes 46), 39–70. Stanford, CA: CSLI Publications.

Kathol, Andreas. 2001. Positional effects in a monostratal grammar of German. *Journal of Linguistics* 37(1). 35–66.

Kaufmann, Ingrid & Dieter Wunderlich. 1998. *Cross-linguistic patterns of resultatives.* SFB 282: Theorie des Lexikons 109. Düsseldorf: Heinrich Heine Uni/BUGH.

Kay, Paul. 2005. Argument structure constructions and the argument-adjunct distinction. In Mirjam Fried & Hans C. Boas (eds.), *Grammatical constructions:*

Back to the roots (Constructional Approaches to Language 4), 71–98. Amsterdam: John Benjamins Publishing Co.

Kay, Paul & Charles J. Fillmore. 1999. Grammatical constructions and linguistic generalizations: The What's X Doing Y? Construction. *Language* 75(1). 1–33.

Kibort, Anna. 2008. On the syntax of ditransitive constructions. In Miriam Butt & Tracy Holloway King (eds.), *Proceedings of the LFG 2008 conference*, 312–332. Stanford, CA: CSLI Publications. http://csli-publications.stanford.edu/LFG/13/, accessed 2018-02-25.

Kiss, Tibor. 1995. *Infinite Komplementation: Neue Studien zum deutschen Verbum infinitum* (Linguistische Arbeiten 333). Tübingen: Max Niemeyer Verlag.

Koenig, Jean-Pierre. 1999. *Lexical relations* (Stanford Monographs in Linguistics). Stanford, CA: CSLI Publications.

Krieger, Hans-Ulrich & John Nerbonne. 1993. Feature-based inheritance networks for computational lexicons. In Ted Briscoe, Ann Copestake & Valeria de Paiva (eds.), *Inheritance, defaults, and the lexicon*, 90–136. Cambridge, UK: Cambridge University Press. A version of this paper is available as DFKI Research Report RR-91-31. Also published in: Proceedings of the ACQUILEX Workshop on Default Inheritance in the Lexicon, Technical Report No. 238, University of Cambridge, Computer Laboratory, October 1991.

Langendoen, D. Terence, Nancy Kalish-Landon & John Dore. 1973. Dative questions: A study in the relation of acceptability to grammaticality of an English sentence type. *Cognition* 4(2). 451–478. DOI:10.1016/0010-0277(73)90004-8

Meurers, Walt Detmar. 1999a. German partial-VP fronting revisited. In Gert Webelhuth, Jean-Pierre Koenig & Andreas Kathol (eds.), *Lexical and Constructional aspects of linguistic explanation* (Studies in Constraint-Based Lexicalism 1), 129–144. Stanford, CA: CSLI Publications.

Meurers, Walt Detmar. 1999b. Raising spirits (and assigning them case). *Groninger Arbeiten zur Germanistischen Linguistik (GAGL)* 43. 173–226. http://www.sfs.uni-tuebingen.de/~dm/papers/gagl99.html, accessed 2018-02-25.

Meurers, Walt Detmar, Gerald Penn & Frank Richter. 2002. A web-based instructional platform for constraint-based grammar formalisms and parsing. In Dragomir Radev & Chris Brew (eds.), *Effective tools and methodologies for teaching NLP and CL*, 18–25. Association for Computational Linguistics. Proceedings of the Workshop held at 40th Annual Meeting of the Association for Computational Linguistics. Philadelphia, PA.

Müller, Stefan. 1996. Complement extraction lexical rules and argument attraction. In Dafydd Gibbon (ed.), *Natural language processing and speech technol-*

ogy: Results of the 3rd KONVENS Conference, Bielefeld, October 1996, 223–236. Berlin: Mouton de Gruyter.

Müller, Stefan. 1999. *Deutsche Syntax deklarativ: Head-Driven Phrase Structure Grammar für das Deutsche* (Linguistische Arbeiten 394). Tübingen: Max Niemeyer Verlag.

Müller, Stefan. 2002. *Complex predicates: Verbal complexes, resultative constructions, and particle verbs in German* (Studies in Constraint-Based Lexicalism 13). Stanford, CA: CSLI Publications.

Müller, Stefan. 2003. Mehrfache Vorfeldbesetzung. *Deutsche Sprache* 31(1). 29–62.

Müller, Stefan. 2006. Phrasal or lexical Constructions? *Language* 82(4). 850–883. DOI:10.1353/lan.2006.0213

Müller, Stefan. 2007a. *Head-Driven Phrase Structure Grammar: Eine Einführung*. 1st edn. (Stauffenburg Einführungen 17). Tübingen: Stauffenburg Verlag.

Müller, Stefan. 2007b. Phrasal or lexical Constructions: Some comments on underspecification of constituent order, compositionality, and control. In Stefan Müller (ed.), *Proceedings of the 14th International Conference on Head-Driven Phrase Structure Grammar*, 373–393. Stanford, CA: CSLI Publications.

Müller, Stefan. 2007c. The Grammix CD Rom: A software collection for developing typed feature structure grammars. In Tracy Holloway King & Emily M. Bender (eds.), *Grammar Engineering across Frameworks 2007* (Studies in Computational Linguistics ONLINE). Stanford, CA: CSLI Publications. http://csli-publications.stanford.edu/GEAF/2007/, accessed 2018-02-25.

Müller, Stefan. 2010a. *Grammatiktheorie* (Stauffenburg Einführungen 20). Tübingen: Stauffenburg Verlag.

Müller, Stefan. 2010b. Persian complex predicates and the limits of inheritance-based analyses. *Journal of Linguistics* 46(3). 601–655. DOI:10.1017/S0022226709990284

Müller, Stefan. 2013a. *Head-Driven Phrase Structure Grammar: Eine Einführung*. 3rd edn. (Stauffenburg Einführungen 17). Tübingen: Stauffenburg Verlag.

Müller, Stefan. 2013b. Unifying everything: Some remarks on Simpler Syntax, Construction Grammar, Minimalism and HPSG. *Language* 89(4). 920–950. DOI:10.1353/lan.2013.0061

Müller, Stefan. 2015a. HPSG – A synopsis. In Tibor Kiss & Artemis Alexiadou (eds.), *Syntax – Theory and analysis: An international handbook* (Handbooks of Linguistics and Communication Science 42.2), 937–973. Berlin: Walter de Gruyter. DOI:10.1515/9783110363708-004

Müller, Stefan. 2015b. The CoreGram project: Theoretical linguistics, theory development and verification. *Journal of Language Modelling* 3(1). 21–86. DOI:10.15398/jlm.v3i1.91

Müller, Stefan. 2016a. *Grammatical theory: From Transformational Grammar to constraint-based approaches* (Textbooks in Language Sciences 1). Berlin: Language Science Press. DOI:10.17169/langsci.b25.167

Müller, Stefan. 2016b. Satztypen: Lexikalisch oder/und phrasal. In Rita Finkbeiner & Jörg Meibauer (eds.), *Satztypen und Konstruktionen im Deutschen* (Linguistik – Impulse und Tendenzen 65), 72–105. Berlin: de Gruyter.

Müller, Stefan. 2017a. Das Lexikon: Wer, wie, was, wieso, weshalb, warum? In Stefan Engelberg, Henning Lobin, Kathrin Steyer & Sascha Wolfer (eds.), *Wortschätze: Dynamik, Muster, Komplexität: Jahrbuch des Instituts für deutsche Sprache*. Berlin: Mouton de Gruyter. DOI:10.1515/9783110579963-002

Müller, Stefan. 2017b. Default inheritance and derivational morphology. In Martijn Wieling, Martin Kroon, Gertjan van Noord & Gosse Bouma (eds.), *From semantics to dialectometry: Festschrift in honor of John Nerbonne* (Tributes 32), 253–262. College Publications.

Müller, Stefan. 2017c. Head-Driven Phrase Structure Grammar, Sign-Based Construction Grammar, and Fluid Construction Grammar: Commonalities and differences. *Constructions and Frames* 9(1). 139–174. DOI:10.1075/cf.9.1.05mul

Müller, Stefan. 2018a. *Germanic syntax*. Ms. Humboldt Universität zu Berlin, to be submitted to Language Science Press. Berlin. https://hpsg.hu-berlin.de/~stefan/Pub/germanic.html, accessed 2018-03-20.

Müller, Stefan. 2018b. *Grammatical theory: From Transformational Grammar to constraint-based approaches*. 2nd edn. (Textbooks in Language Sciences 1). Berlin: Language Science Press. DOI:10.5281/zenodo.1193241

Müller, Stefan & Bjarne Ørsnes. 2013. Towards an HPSG analysis of object shift in Danish. In Glyn Morrill & Mark-Jan Nederhof (eds.), *Formal Grammar: 17th and 18th International Conferences, FG 2012, Opole, Poland, August 2012, revised selected papers, FG 2013, Düsseldorf, Germany, August 2013: Proceedings* (Lecture Notes in Computer Science 8036), 69–89. Berlin: Springer Verlag.

Müller, Stefan & Stephen Mark Wechsler. 2014a. Lexical approaches to argument structure. *Theoretical Linguistics* 40(1–2). 1–76. DOI:10.1515/tl-2014-0001

Müller, Stefan & Stephen Mark Wechsler. 2014b. Two sides of the same slim Boojum: Further arguments for a lexical approach to argument structure. *Theoretical Linguistics* 40(1–2). 187–224. DOI:10.1515/tl-2014-0009

Müller, Stefan & Stephen Mark Wechsler. 2015. The lexical-constructional debate. In *Word meaning and syntax: Approaches to the interface* (Oxford Surveys in Syntax and Morphology 9), 228–279. Oxford: Oxford University Press.

Nerbonne, John. 1986. 'Phantoms' and German fronting: Poltergeist constituents? *Linguistics* 24(5). 857–870. DOI:10.1515/ling.1986.24.5.857

Penn, Gerald. 2004. Balancing clarity and efficiency in typed feature logic through delaying. In Donia Scott (ed.), *Proceedings of the 42nd Meeting of the Association for Computational Linguistics (ACL'04), main volume*, 239–246. Barcelona, Spain.

Pollard, Carl J. & Andrew M. Moshier. 1990. Unifying partial descriptions of sets. In Philip P. Hanson (ed.), *Information, language and cognition* (Vancouver Studies in Cognitive Science 1), 285–322. Vancouver: University of British Columbia Press.

Pollard, Carl J. & Ivan A. Sag. 1987. *Information-based syntax and semantics* (CSLI Lecture Notes 13). Stanford, CA: CSLI Publications.

Pollard, Carl J. & Ivan A. Sag. 1994. *Head-Driven Phrase Structure Grammar* (Studies in Contemporary Linguistics). Chicago: The University of Chicago Press.

Przepiórkowski, Adam. 1999. On case assignment and "adjuncts as complements". In Gert Webelhuth, Jean-Pierre Koenig & Andreas Kathol (eds.), *Lexical and Constructional aspects of linguistic explanation* (Studies in Constraint-Based Lexicalism 1), 231–245. Stanford, CA: CSLI Publications.

Rizzi, Luigi. 1997. The fine structure of the left periphery. In Liliane Haegeman (ed.), *Elements of grammar*, 281–337. Dordrecht: Kluwer Academic Publishers.

Roberts, Ian. 1988. Thematic minimality. *Rivista di Grammatica Generativa* 13. 111–137.

Sag, Ivan A. 1997. English relative clause constructions. *Journal of Linguistics* 33(2). 431–484.

Sag, Ivan A. 2010. English filler-gap constructions. *Language* 86(3). 486–545.

Sag, Ivan A. 2012. Sign-Based Construction Grammar: An informal synopsis. In Hans C. Boas & Ivan A. Sag (eds.), *Sign-based Construction Grammar* (CSLI Lecture Notes 193), 69–202. Stanford, CA: CSLI Publications.

Sag, Ivan A., Hans C. Boas & Paul Kay. 2012. Introducing Sign-Based Construction Grammar. In Hans C. Boas & Ivan A. Sag (eds.), *Sign-based Construction Grammar* (CSLI Lecture Notes 193), 1–29. Stanford, CA: CSLI Publications.

Sheinfux, Livnat Herzig, Nurit Melnik & Shuly Wintner. 2016. Representing argument structure. *Journal of Linguistics* 53(4). 1–50. DOI:10.1017/S0022226716000189

Simpson, Jane. 1983. Resultatives. In Lori S. Levin, Malka Rappaport & Annie Zaenen (eds.), *Papers in Lexical Functional Grammar*, 143–157. Indiana: Indiana University Linguistics Club. Reprint: Simpson (2005).

Simpson, Jane. 2005. Resultatives. In Miriam Butt & Tracy Holloway King (eds.), *Lexical semantics in LFG*, 149–161. Stanford, CA: CSLI Publications.

Steels, Luc (ed.). 2011. *Design patterns in Fluid Construction Grammar* (Constructional Approaches to Language 11). Amsterdam: John Benjamins Publishing Co. DOI:10.1075/cal.11

Toivonen, Ida. 2013. English benefactive NPs. In Miriam Butt & Tracy Holloway King (eds.), *Proceedings of the LFG 2013 conference*, 503–523. Stanford, CA: CSLI Publications.

Tomasello, Michael. 2000. Do young children have adult syntactic competence? *Cognition* 74(3). 209–253.

Tomasello, Michael. 2003. *Constructing a language: A usage-based theory of language acquisition*. Cambridge, MA: Harvard University Press.

Tungseth, Mai. 2007. Interactions of particles, adjectival resultatives and benefactive double object constructions in Norwegian. *Nordic Journal of Linguistics* 30(2). 209–228. DOI:10.1017/S033258650700176X

Uszkoreit, Hans. 1987. *Word order and constituent structure in German* (CSLI Lecture Notes 8). Stanford, CA: CSLI Publications.

van Trijp, Remi. 2011. A design pattern for argument structure constructions. In Luc Steels (ed.), *Design patterns in Fluid Construction Grammar* (Constructional Approaches to Language 11), 115–145. Amsterdam: John Benjamins Publishing Co. DOI:10.1075/cal.11.07tri

Verspoor, Cornelia Maria. 1997. *Contextually-dependent lexical semantics*. University of Edinburgh dissertation.

Wechsler, Stephen Mark. 1991. *Argument structure and linking*. Stanford University dissertation.

Wechsler, Stephen Mark. 1997. Resultative predicates and control. In Ralph C. Blight & Michelle J. Moosally (eds.), *Texas Linguistic Forum 38: The syntax and semantics of predication: Proceedings of the 1997 Texas Linguistics Society Conference*, 307–321. Austin, Texas: University of Texas, Department of Linguistics.

Wechsler, Stephen Mark & Bokyung Noh. 2001. On resultative predicates and clauses: Parallels between Korean and English. *Language Sciences* 23(4). 391–423.

Wunderlich, Dieter. 1992. *CAUSE and the structure of verbs*. Arbeiten des SFB 282 No. 36. Düsseldorf/Wuppertal: Heinrich Heine Uni/BUGH.

Wunderlich, Dieter. 1997. Argument extension by lexical adjunction. *Journal of Semantics* 14(2). 95–142. DOI:10.1093/jos/14.2.95

Yip, Moira, Joan Maling & Ray S. Jackendoff. 1987. Case in tiers. *Language* 63(2). 217–250. DOI:10.2307/415655

Zaenen, Annie & Ronald M. Kaplan. 2002. Subsumption and equality: German partial fronting in LFG. In Miriam Butt & Tracy Holloway King (eds.), *Proceedings of the LFG 2002 conference*. Stanford, CA: CSLI Publications. http://csli-publications.stanford.edu/LFG/7/, accessed 2018-02-25.

Name index

www.ingramcontent.com/pod-product-compliance
Lightning Source LLC
Chambersburg PA
CBHW050921150426
42812CB00051B/1931
* 9 7 8 3 9 6 1 1 0 1 2 2 1 *